Helen Hadkins, Samantha Lewis and Joanna Budden

Interactive

Student's Book 3 with Web Zone access

CAMBRIDGE
UNIVERSITY PRESS

Contents

Graphic Novel

Culture UK South Wales

Culture World The Arctic

Song Friendship Train

Graphic Novel

Culture UK Birmingham

	Grammar	Vocabulary	Interaction, Speaking and Pronunciation	Listening, Reading and Portfolio	
7 That's incredible!	Modal verbs of deduction: present • Modal verbs of deduction: past	Extreme adjectives • Phrasal verbs with *go*	*Interaction 7*: Guessing what happened • *Speak*: Guess what the picture is • *Pronunciation*: Elision of *have*	*Read*: Mothman and the Men in Black • *Listen*: Strange stories • *Portfolio 7*: A mystery story	Culture World The Bahamas
8 Gaming and gadgets	Quantifiers review • Non-defining relative clauses	Health problems • Technology	*Interaction 8*: Asking for and giving explanations • *Speak*: Talking about your opinions • *Pronunciation*: Words with *ough*	*Read*: Active gaming • *Listen*: Gadgets • *Portfolio 8*: A formal letter of complaint	Song Zeroes and Ones

Review 7 and 8 Grammar Vocabulary Correct it! How are you doing?

	Grammar	Vocabulary	Interaction, Speaking and Pronunciation	Listening, Reading and Portfolio	
9 Seeing is believing	*as if, as though* and *like* • *a/an, the* or no article	Adjectives of opinion • Truth and lies	*Interaction 9*: Being tactful • *Speak*: Speculating on photos • *Pronunciation*: The sounds /ð/ and /θ/	*Read*: The camera never lies • *Listen*: Art • *Portfolio 9*: Writing about your opinions	Graphic Novel
10 Beyond words	Reported statements • Reported questions, commands and requests	Reading materials • Adverbs and adverbial phrases	*Interaction 10*: Checking details • *Speak*: Talking about your reading habits • *Pronunciation*: Rhythm	*Read*: Rapping Shakespeare • *Listen*: Interviews about reading habits • *Portfolio 10*: A book review	Culture UK Edinburgh

Review 9 and 10 Grammar Vocabulary Correct it! How are you doing?

	Grammar	Vocabulary	Interaction, Speaking and Pronunciation	Listening, Reading and Portfolio	
11 Is it a crime?	Subject and object questions • *wish* and *if only*	Crime • Crime collocations	*Interaction 11*: Apologising • *Speak*: Discussing crimes and punishments • *Pronunciation*: Consonant clusters at the ends of words	*Read*: Computer criminals • *Listen*: Crime quiz show • *Portfolio 11*: A report	Culture World Singapore
12 Moving on	*would rather* and *would prefer* • Third conditional	Hopes and ambitions • Dependent prepositions	*Interaction 12*: Dealing with a problem • *Speak*: Talking about preferences • *Pronunciation*: Sentence stress	*Read*: Aim High • *Listen*: The end of the school year • *Portfolio 12*: A record of achievement	Song It Ain't Over 'Til It's Over

Review 11 and 12 Grammar Vocabulary Correct it! How are you doing?

Skills4Real: Units 1–4	*Skills4Real: Units 5–8*	*Skills4Real: Units 9–12*	*Interaction: Student A*
Interaction: Student B	*Speaking activities*	*Wordlist* *Irregular verbs*	*Phonemic chart*

1 Get up and go!

Present tense review
Past tense review
Vocabulary: Fitness; Phrasal verbs
and expressions with *get*
Interaction 1: Catching up with a friend

1 Read and listen

a Read the text quickly and match the headings
with the paragraphs 1–4.

History   Music   What is capoeira?   Moves

1 ....

A sport? A passion? A way of life? Capoeira is not easy to define, but this beautiful and energetic combination of martial arts, music and dance is growing fast. Capoeira schools have opened all over the world and more and more people are doing capoeira. So why has this Brazilian art form become so popular?

2 ....

Capoeira is a 'game' where two players move around inside a circle. Players kick to attack each other and stretch or fall on the ground to try to escape, but the most important move is the 'ginga' which means 'to swing'. Players swing backwards and forwards to the rhythm of the music and, because they are constantly moving, it is harder for opponents to attack. Capoeira is such an intense form of exercise that players must warm up before they start training, so that they are flexible enough to do the moves.

3 ....

The music and instruments make capoeira different to other physical activities, and without them capoeira wouldn't be so unusual. The main instrument, the 'berimbau', is a strange-looking object consisting of a curved piece of wood and one string. The musicians sing songs in Portuguese and the lyrics tell stories about life. Some of the songs have been passed from generation to generation, but new songs are being created all the time.

4 ....

If you really want to understand capoeira, it's important to know about its history. Over 400 years ago, African slaves were taken to Brazil to work on sugar and tobacco plantations. They took their music, culture and beliefs with them, and capoeira was one of the things that helped them keep their African identity. They also wanted to be strong and fit so that they could get away from their masters. They played music to hide the fact that they were training and, as a result, slave masters thought the slaves were dancing for fun, not getting fit in order to run away. So what is capoeira? Perhaps the best way to understand it is to try it yourself.

b 🔊 **1.2** Read the text again and listen. Are the sentences *right* (✓), *wrong* (✗) or *doesn't say* (–)? Correct the wrong sentences.

1 A lot of people in different countries are doing capoeira.
2 Capoeira is mainly popular with women.
3 When players do the 'ginga' they fall on the ground.
4 Players can't do capoeira without warming up.
5 All the capoeira songs are very old.
6 Slave masters didn't know the real reason why slaves practised capoeira.

c Find the words in the text that mean ...

1 explain the meaning of something (para 1)
2 two or more different things together (para 1)
3 move smoothly backwards and forwards (para 2)
4 people who belong to someone else and have to work for them (para 4)
5 things you believe are true (para 4)

d Work in a group. Answer the questions.

1 Have you tried any kind of dance or martial art? Did you enjoy it? Why? / Why not?
2 What types of dance or martial arts would you like to try? Why?

(2) Grammar

Present tense review

a Look at the examples and match them with the tenses.

> present simple (x2)   present continuous
> present perfect (x2)
>
> 1 Capoeira schools **have opened** all over the world.
> 2 More and more people **are doing** capoeira.
> 3 Capoeira **is not** easy to define.
> 4 Players **kick** to attack each other.
> 5 Why **has** this art form **become** so popular?
>
> (Circle) the correct words to complete the rules.
> We use:
>
> ● the **present simple / present continuous** for facts.
> ● the **present simple / present continuous** for habits and routines.
> ● the **present simple / present continuous** for actions happening now.
> ● the **present simple / present perfect** for actions which happened at some time in the past.
> ● the **present continuous / present perfect** for actions that started in the past and continue in the present.

Grammar reference: Workbook page 76

b Complete the sentences with the correct present form of the verbs.

1 He .... (do) sport every day.
2 What's that noise? Someone .... (play) the drums.
3 .... you ever .... (try) capoeira?
4 I .... (not know) the answer. Can you help me?
5 She .... (not wear) her school uniform today because it's Sunday.
6 Alana .... (never visit) Brazil.

> **Check it out!**
>
> ● Some verbs are not usually used in the continuous form: *agree*, *be*, *believe*, *hate*, *like*, *need*, *remember*, *understand*, *want*.
> I **agree** with you. NOT I'm agreeing with you.

c Complete the text with the correct present form of the verbs.

> be   become   not know   open   play   want

Belly dancing and Darbuka

¹ .... you .... to get fit and have fun, but you ² .... what to do? Well, why don't you learn belly dancing or, just for fun, the Darbuka? Belly dancing ³ .... great exercise for everyone, and it ⁴ .... more and more popular around the world. Or you could learn to play the Darbuka, the Arabic drum which people ⁵ .... during belly-dancing classes. A new fun fitness centre ⁶ .... in the town centre recently, so if you are looking for a new hobby, come and find us!

d Work with a partner. Tell him/her about …

1 something you do every day.
2 something interesting you've done recently.
3 something new you're learning this year.

(3) Speak

a Match the two parts of the questions.

1 What's the best
2 When do you feel
3 What exercise have
4 Which sports clubs or gyms
5 Are you training
6 Do you think you have
7 Which new sports would

A most active? In the morning? At night?
B enough time for sport? Why? / Why not?
C for anything at the moment?
D have you been to?
E type of exercise?
F you like to try? Why?
G you done this week?

b Work in a group. Answer the questions.

c Tell the class about your group. Who likes/doesn't like doing exercise? Who's the most/least active? What types of exercise are the most popular?

(4) Vocabulary

Fitness

a 🔊 **1.3** Match the words with the definitions. Then listen and check.

> **1** active **2** energetic **3** fit **4** flexible
> **5** stretch **6** train **7** warm up **8** work out

A do lots of exercise to prepare for a sports event

B do exercise in a gym to make your body fit and strong

C make your arms, legs or body straight or long

D do some exercises to get ready before you do a sport

E able to bend your body easily into different positions

F having lots of energy

G healthy and strong, as a result of regular exercise

H always busy doing things and moving around

b Do you know any more words to do with fitness? Write them down.

c Circle the correct words.

This year I've joined an aerobics class because I wanted to be more ¹ *stretch / active* and feel healthier. At the beginning of each class we ² *warm up / work out* and we ³ *train / stretch* so that we don't hurt our muscles. Then we spend about 45 minutes ⁴ *working out / warming up*. I found it hard at first because I wasn't very ⁵ *fit / train*, but it's easier now, and I'm definitely more ⁶ *stretch / flexible*. Even if I'm tired before the class, I always feel ⁷ *work out / energetic* afterwards. Aerobics is a good way to ⁸ *stretch / train* if you want to become strong and healthy.

d Work with a partner. Answer the questions.

1 What do you do to keep fit?

2 Which sports do you think you need the most energy to do? Why?

3 Which sports do you need to be flexible to do? Why?

(5) Listen

a Look at the photo. What sport are the people doing? Who do you think they are?

b 🔊 **1.4** Listen and number the events in Matthew's life.

He joined a martial arts club. ☐

He travels the world with the Shaolin monks. ☐

He saw the Shaolin monks in London. ☐

He went to China. ☐

c 🔊 **1.4** Listen again and answer the questions.

1 How old was Matthew when he decided to become a Shaolin monk?

2 Why didn't Matthew's parents want him to go to China?

3 How many hours of training did he do every day in China?

4 Who does Matthew want to help?

Culture Vulture

Did you know that all students in Britain have to do Physical Education (PE) at school until they are 16? Do you have to do PE at school? Do you think PE should be compulsory at school?

6 Pronunciation 🔵DVD

/ɪz/

a 🔊 **1.5** Sometimes we pronounce -*s*, -*es* or the possessive *'s* as /ɪz/. Listen to these words with the /ɪz/ sound. Add -*s*, -*es* or the possessive *'s*.

1 house..**S**..
2 class.......
3 exercise.......
4 wash.......
5 stretch.......
6 George.......

b 🔊 **1.6** Tick (✓) the words that end in the syllable /ɪz/. Then listen, check and repeat.

1 dances
2 Matthew's
3 chooses
4 shows
5 Chris's
6 messages
7 drinks
8 teaches
9 sports
10 fishes

c 🔊 **1.7** Listen and repeat.

> *Jess sends messages about dances and exercises to George's phone during Chris's classes.*

7 Grammar

Past tense review

a Look at the examples and match them with the structures in the box.

> past continuous   past simple (x2)   used to
>
> 1 *He **joined** a martial arts club.*
> 2 *While he **was watching** he decided to become a monk.*
> 3 *He **used to train** every day before school.*
> 4 *He **didn't understand** the language.*
>
> Ⓒircle the correct words to complete the rules.
>
> ● We use the **past simple** / **past continuous** for an action in progress at a particular time in the past.
> ● We use the **past simple** / **past continuous** for a completed action in the past or a situation in the past.
> ● We use **the past continuous** / ***used to*** for a repeated action or situation in the past which is not true now.

Grammar reference: Workbook page 78

Check it out!

● The negative and question form of ***used to*** is **use to**.
   She **didn't use to like** vegetables.
   NOT ~~She didn't used to like vegetables~~.
   Did you **use to get up** early?
   NOT ~~Did you used to get up early?~~

b Ⓒircle the correct words. Sometimes both answers are possible.

Energy drinks first ¹ *became / were becoming* popular in the 1980s and 1990s. At first, only athletes ² *were drinking / used to drink* them for extra energy before and during workouts or training. Then, more and more people ³ *discovered / used to discover* them and soon everyone ⁴ *started / was starting* to drink them. People often ⁵ *drank / used to drink* them while they ⁶ *did / were doing* exercise or when they ⁷ *used to need / needed* an energy boost. However, today experts say that too many energy drinks are bad for you.

c Complete the sentences with the correct past form of the verbs. Use *used to* where possible.

1 I ....(learn) to swim when I ....(be) five.
2 We ....(play) tennis every week, but now we only play once a month.
3 I ....(see) my friend Pete when I ....(run) in the park yesterday.
4 Where ....you..............(go) last night? I ....(not know) where you..............(be).
5 He ....(want) to do some exercise so he ....(join) a gym and ....(start) to work out every day.
6 She ....(not be) very fit, but now she's a fitness instructor.

d Work with a partner. Tell him/her about ...

1 something you used to do when you were younger.
2 something you saw while you were coming to school this morning.
3 something you got for your last birthday.

(8) Vocabulary

Phrasal verbs and expressions with *get*

a 🔊 1.8 Match the phrasal verbs with the meanings. Then listen and check.

1 His parents wanted him to **get into** university.
2 I hope I **get through** this aerobics class!
3 It's difficult to **get** your message **across**.
4 I **get on with** my sister. We're great friends.
5 I must **get on with** my homework.
6 Some people try to **get out of** PE.

A avoid doing something you should do
B be chosen to go to a university or to join a sports team
C come to the end of a difficult time
D communicate an idea to someone
E continue doing something, especially work
F like and be friends with someone

b Replace the underlined words with the correct form of the phrasal verbs in Exercise 8a.

1 You always try and <u>avoid</u> tidying your room.
2 I've <u>come to the end of</u> my exams.
3 Do you <u>like</u> many people in your class?
4 She <u>was chosen for</u> the school hockey team.
5 I can't <u>communicate</u> my idea to him.
6 I must <u>continue with</u> my work now.

c Match the uses of *get* in the expressions with the meanings 1–4.

1 obtain	2 become	3 receive	4 arrive

A What was his life like when he **got** to China?
B Little by little he **got** fitter and stronger.
C Where did you **get** the information from?
D She **got** lots of presents for her birthday.

d What does *get* mean in these expressions?

arrive	become	obtain	receive

1 get a present   *receive*
2 get home   ....
3 get a text message ....
4 get the shopping ....
5 get an email   ....
6 get older   ....
7 get tired   ....
8 get to school   ....

e Work with a partner.
Student A: Complete the questions with the correct form of the phrasal verbs and expressions. Then ask and answer the questions.
Student B: Turn to page 124.

get better   get home   get on with   get tired
get to school

1 What do you usually do when you .... from school?
2 Which subject at school would you like to .... at?
3 Do you .... if you stay up too late?
4 Have you ever .... late in the morning?
5 What time do you usually .... your homework?

Interaction 1 📀 DVD

Catching up with a friend

A ☐   B ☐   C ☐
D ☐   E ☐   F ☐

a 🔊 1.9 Listen to the conversation between Mickey and Jessica. Tick (✓) the sports that are mentioned.

b 🔊 1.9 Listen again and match the questions or phrases with the responses.

1 How's it going?   A Lots of things.
2 How are things?   B Great.
3 So what's new?   C Nothing really.
4 What have you been up to? D Yeah, catch you later.
5 Anyway, I've got to go now. E Fine, thanks.
6 See you around.   F Yeah, me too.

c Work with a partner.
Student A: Turn to page 118.
Student B: Turn to page 121.

Portfolio 1

An informal article

a Read Keira's article for the school website. Does she enjoy keeping fit now?

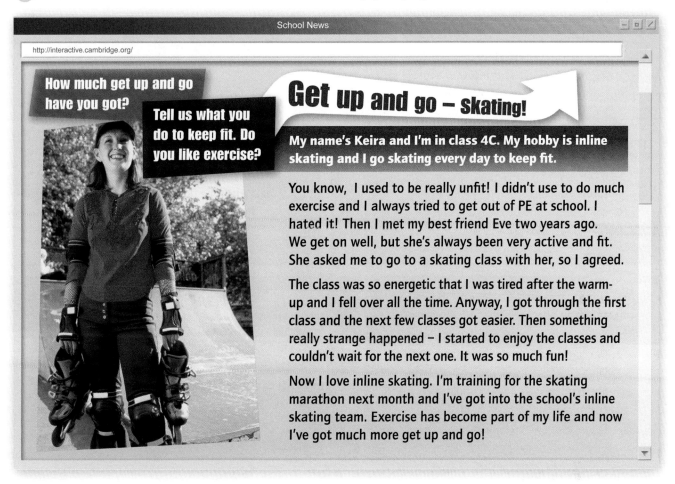

School News

http://interactive.cambridge.org/

How much get up and go have you got?

Tell us what you do to keep fit. Do you like exercise?

Get up and go – Skating!

My name's Keira and I'm in class 4C. My hobby is inline skating and I go skating every day to keep fit.

You know, I used to be really unfit! I didn't use to do much exercise and I always tried to get out of PE at school. I hated it! Then I met my best friend Eve two years ago. We get on well, but she's always been very active and fit. She asked me to go to a skating class with her, so I agreed.

The class was so energetic that I was tired after the warm-up and I fell over all the time. Anyway, I got through the first class and the next few classes got easier. Then something really strange happened – I started to enjoy the classes and couldn't wait for the next one. It was so much fun!

Now I love inline skating. I'm training for the skating marathon next month and I've got into the school's inline skating team. Exercise has become part of my life and now I've got much more get up and go!

b Read the article again and answer the questions.
1 What is the title?
2 Who is the reader?
3 How many paragraphs has Keira written?
4 What information has she included in each paragraph?

c Find words in the article that make the tone informal and friendly. Look for contractions, phrasal verbs and informal expressions.
You know, I used to be really unfit!
We get on well.

> ## Check it out!
>
> **When writing an article:**
> - include a title
> - talk to your reader (your classmates, your teacher or a friend)
> - be friendly (use contractions, phrasal verbs and informal expressions)
> - talk about your experience
> - organise your ideas into paragraphs

d Read the announcement and write an article for the school website. Use the Check it out! box to help you.

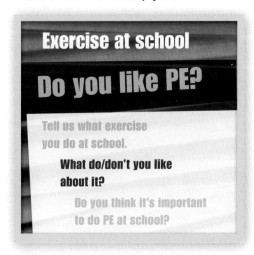

Exercise at school

Do you like PE?

Tell us what exercise you do at school.

What do/don't you like about it?

Do you think it's important to do PE at school?

e Work with a partner. Read your partner's article. Is it interesting? Does he/she sound informal and friendly? Why? / Why not?

CRASH

1.10

THE SCHOOL TRIP WAS OVER. IT WAS TIME TO START THE LONG JOURNEY HOME.

ALI, BEN, LEE AND LAURA WERE ON THE PLANE WHEN A STORM BEGAN.

WHAT'S HAPPENING?! HELP!

EVERYBODY GET READY. I'M GOING TO MAKE AN EMERGENCY LANDING. HOLD ON TIGHT!

CRUNCH

HELLO, CAN ANYBODY HEAR ME? WE NEED HELP. HELLO? HELLO?

WHAT HAPPENED? AAGH! MY LEG!

IT'S NO USE, LEE. THE RADIO MUST BE BROKEN.

HMM. MAYBE WE CAN CALL SOMEONE ON OUR MOBILES.

I'VE BEEN TRYING BUT THERE'S NO SIGNAL.

SO WHAT ARE WE GOING TO DO? WE NEED TO GET HELP FOR MARK. HE'S REALLY BADLY HURT.

BUT WE CAN'T LEAVE HIM ALONE, BEN.

LISTEN, ALI. THE BEST THING IS TO LEAVE ME AND GET HELP. I THINK I'VE BROKEN MY LEG. IF I COME WITH YOU, I'LL MAKE EVERYBODY GO TOO SLOWLY.

WHERE SHOULD WE GO? WE'RE IN THE MIDDLE OF NOWHERE. WHAT DO YOU THINK, LAURA?

WE SHOULD GO DOWNHILL AND LOOK FOR A RIVER. IF WE FIND ONE, WE CAN FOLLOW IT TO A VILLAGE.

BUT WHAT IF SOMEONE COMES LOOKING FOR US?

NOBODY WILL, BECAUSE NOBODY KNOWS WE'RE HERE. YOU HAVE TO GO.

THEY SET OFF THROUGH THE FOREST ...

IT'S GETTING TOO DARK TO SEE WHERE WE'RE GOING, AND I'M REALLY COLD AND WET. WE SHOULD STOP SOMEWHERE.

WE CAN'T STOP, BEN. WE NEED TO GET HELP FOR MARK.

BEN'S RIGHT, LEE. WE NEED TO REST FOR A WHILE. LET'S GO IN THAT CAVE.

GOOD IDEA, LAURA. WE CAN WAIT HERE UNTIL THE STORM FINISHES.

SHOULD WE GO IN? IT'S VERY DARK. WHAT IF THERE'S A BEAR OR SOMETHING?

IF THERE IS, WE'LL HAVE TO DEAL WITH IT.

WHAT'S THAT OVER THERE?

WHAT?

I CAN SEE SOMETHING STRANGE. IT SAYS 'PLEASE HELP US'.

please help us

SOMEONE'S BEEN HERE BEFORE US.

WHAT'S THAT LIGHT?

THERE'S SOMEONE THERE!

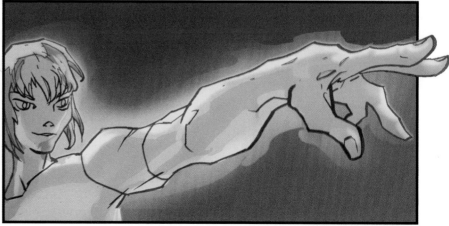

2 Waste not, want not

Present perfect with *just* / *yet* / *already*
Present perfect continuous
Vocabulary: Electrical items; Prefixes
Interaction 2: Returning items to a shop

1 Vocabulary Electrical items

a 🔊 1.11 Match the words with the pictures. Then listen and check.

1 dishwasher   2 electric razor
3 food processor   4 freezer   5 hairdryer
6 microwave   7 toaster   8 tumble dryer
9 vacuum cleaner   10 washing machine

(A)

(B)

(C)

(D)

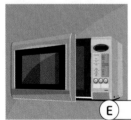
(E)

(F)

(G)

(H)

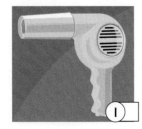
(I)

(J)

b Put the words in Exercise 1a into the word webs.

dishwasher

cooking   cleaning   other

c Do you know any more words for electrical items? Write them down.

d Which do you think are the three most useful electrical items? Choose your 'top three' and then compare with your partner.

⋯⋯➤ A: *I think the washing machine is the most useful. It saves a lot of time.*
B: *Yes, but I think the hairdryer is more useful. You can use it for drying and styling your hair.*

2 Pronunciation

Stress patterns

a 🔊 1.12 Listen to the stress patterns in these words.

two syllables   ● ● toaster   ● ● machine

three syllables   ● ● ● hairdryer   ● ● ● computer

b Put the words in the correct column.

dishwasher   guitar   umbrella   ~~freezer~~   police
firefighter   money   recycle   potato   island
timetable   repair

● ●	● ●	● ● ●	● ● ●
freezer			

c 🔊 1.13 Listen, check and repeat.

d Work with a partner. Your partner closes his/her book. Write a word from Exercise 2b. Can your partner remember how many syllables it has and where the stress is?

③ Read and listen

a Look at the picture and guess the answers to the questions.

What is this sculpture made of?   Why do you think it was built?   Who do think made it?

b Read the text quickly and see if your guesses in Exercise 3a were correct.

The wonderful world of WEEE

This giant monster is a sculpture created by Paul Bonomini. It's called the WEEE Man. WEEE stands for 'Waste Electrical and Electronic Equipment', also known as 'e-waste'. Paul Bonomini wanted to show how much electrical waste a normal person in the UK generates in an average lifetime of 77 years. The average family in Britain owns 25 electrical items and each person generates 517 kg of rubbish each year. Only 104 kg are recycled and the rest goes to landfill sites. The WEEE Man weighs 3.3 tonnes (3,300 kg), which is the amount of e-waste produced by the average person in their lifetime. That's the equivalent of the weight of three cars.

If e-waste isn't recycled, it sits in landfill sites and the toxic material goes into the ground and contaminates the earth. So, why do we produce so much waste anyway? Well, have you ever tried to repair your broken printer or camera? In many places it can be difficult, as most electrical repair shops have disappeared. Even if you find a shop to repair your old goods, it often costs more to repair something like a washing machine or toaster than to throw it away and buy a new one!

The WEEE Man now lives at the Eden Project, an environmental centre in Cornwall, in the southwest of England. Thousands of people have already visited the WEEE Man and seen for themselves just how much e-waste one human being can create. The seven-metre-tall sculpture has really made a big impression on everyone who has seen it. It has also inspired other artists to make sculptures out of e-waste. In fact, the Czech Republic has held a competition for artists to create dinosaurs from e-waste and the results were wonderful.

Since the WEEE Man was 'born', the problems we have with disposing of e-waste haven't disappeared and we haven't found a real solution yet. We can't ban e-waste, but things are getting better. Many countries have just introduced new laws to force the manufacturers of electrical goods to recycle old items. But have we already created too much waste?

c 🔊 **1.14** Read the text again and listen. Then answer the questions.

1 What do the numbers in the text refer to: 77, 25, 517, 3,300 and 7?
2 What does Paul Bonomini want people to think about when they see his sculpture?
3 Give two reasons why it can be difficult to repair electrical appliances.
4 Give an example of how one country has been inspired by the WEEE Man.
5 What have many countries done recently to try and solve the problem of e-waste?

d Find the words in the text that mean …

1 typical or usual (para 1)
2 places where waste is put in the ground (para 2)
3 makes something dirty or poisonous (para 2)
4 relating to the environment (para 3)
5 prohibit or not allow (para 4)
6 companies that produce something (para 4)

e Work in a group. Answer the questions.

1 Is it possible to recycle e-waste in your town? If so, how?
2 What things do you recycle and reuse?
3 Do you think recycling is important? Why? / Why not?

Culture Vulture

Did you know that some regions in the UK give rewards to residents who recycle a lot of waste? They weigh the waste and residents win points. The points can be exchanged for things like cinema tickets. Do you think it's a good idea? Are there any similar schemes where you live?

(4) Grammar

Present perfect with *just/yet/already*

a Look at the examples. Then (circle) the correct words to complete the rules.

> *Thousands of people have **already** visited the WEEE Man.*
> *Have we **already** created too much waste?*
> *Many countries have **just** introduced new laws.*
> *Have you **just** arrived?*
> *We haven't found a real solution **yet**.*
> *Has he seen the WEEE Man **yet**?*

- We use **already / just** to mean 'sooner than expected'.
- We use **yet / just** to mean 'a short time ago'.
- We use **already / yet** to mean 'until now'.

- *Already* and *just* usually go **before / after** the past participle.
- *Yet* is usually used in **positive / negative** sentences and questions, and goes at the end.

Grammar reference: Workbook page 76

b Put the words in the correct order.

1 haven't / yet / my / bike / repaired / I
2 heard / the / have / I / news / good / just
3 booked / We / flights / already / the / have
4 yet / seen / WEEE / Man / Have / you / the ?
5 just / a / phone / She / bought / has / mobile / new.
6 Have / that / you / film / seen / already ?
7 tickets / the / haven't / got / for / yet / They / concert

c Complete the responses with the present perfect and the words in brackets.

1 A: Would you like something to drink?
   B: No thanks, I _____ a glass of water.
      (just / have)

2 A: Are your parents going to give you a new mobile?
   B: I don't know. They _____ . (not decide / yet)

3 A: What do you think about the new Super Mario game?
   B: It's a bit too easy. I _____ level 3 and I only got it yesterday. (already / pass)

4 A: Where's Luis?
   B: He went to take the recycling to the containers but he _____ . (not come back / yet)

d Work in a group. Ask each other what you've done this week. Use the ideas in the box or your own. Use *just*, *already* and *yet*.

> homework / go to the cinema / have a class / have exams / watch TV / go shopping / play sport

A: *Have you done your homework yet?*
B: *No, but I've already had three exams.*
C: *I've just played basketball but I haven't done my homework yet!*

Check it out!

- **Been** and **gone** have different meanings.
  She's been to Brazil = She went to Brazil in the past, but she isn't there now.
  She's gone to Brazil = She's in Brazil now.

(5) Speak

a Work with a partner. Use the language to ask questions.

Have you ...

bought
had
thrown away
lost

a computer?
more than 2 mobile phones?
more than 2 MP3 players?
an electrical item?

When?
Where?
Why?
What?

b Tell the class two things about your partner.

> *Monica has had three mobile phones.*

6 Vocabulary

Prefixes

a Look at the words in the table. What do the prefixes mean? Put the words in the box in the correct columns.

| too much | ~~again~~ | before | not enough/below | better |

re- *again*	over-	under-	pre-	super-
recharge reuse retake	oversleep overweight overpriced	underpaid under-age underground	precooked preheat pre-paid	supermodel superpower supermarket

b 📢 **1.15** Choose the correct word from Exercise 6a to complete the sentences. Then listen and check.

1 She's just started doing photo shoots for magazines and she wants to be a .... one day.
2 He can't go into the disco. He's only 17 so he's ....
3 I try to .... the plastic bags I get from the supermarket.
4 Someone who is too heavy is ....
5 I've just bought a .... mobile phone. I can only use the minutes I've already paid for.
6 I've got to .... my laptop. The battery is dead.
7 You don't need to make dinner. You can buy lots of .... meals at our local ....
8 When I study late at night I sometimes .... the next morning and don't get to school until 11:00.

c Do you know any more words with the prefixes in Exercise 6a? Write them in the table.

d Work with a partner. Answer the questions.

1 When was the last time you overslept?
2 Do you think computer games are overpriced?
3 Are part-time jobs for teenagers underpaid in your country?
4 Have you ever retaken an exam?
5 What things do you reuse?

7 Listen

a 📢 **1.16** Listen to John Black talking about a time bank. Tick (✓) the things he mentions.

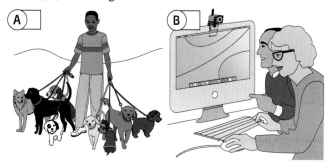

b 📢 **1.16** Listen again. Choose the correct answer: A, B or C.

1 What do members of the time bank earn?
  A money   **B** time credits   **C** food
2 What is Bill an expert in?
  A music   **B** dog walking   **C** computers
3 What has Bill been learning to do?
  A play the guitar   **B** speak Spanish   **C** paint
4 How old is the youngest member of the time bank?
  A 13   **B** 18   **C** 16
5 What is Josh good at looking after?
  A young children   **B** old people   **C** pets

c Work in a group. Answer the questions.

1 Do you think that time banking is a good idea? Why? / Why not?
2 What could you offer to do if you joined a time bank?

(8) Grammar

Present perfect continuous

a Look at the examples. Then (circle) the correct words to complete the rules.

> ....> He **'s been learning** to play the guitar with Amrit.
> **Have** you **been banking** many time credits yourself recently?
> Josh **hasn't been doing** it for long.

- We use the present perfect continuous for actions which started in the past and have finished **recently / a long time ago** or are still continuing.
- We form the present perfect continuous with *has/ have(n't)* + *been* + **verb + -ing / infinitive**.

Grammar reference: Workbook page 79

Check it out!

- *for* + a period of time
  I've been learning English **for** ten years.
- *since* + a specific point in time
  I've been waiting for you **since** 8 o'clock.

b Complete the sentences with the correct verbs in the present perfect continuous.

ask	dream	not go	not learn	watch	work

1 You look really tired, I think you .... too hard recently.

2 I .... Spanish for very long so I'm not very good at speaking.

3 .... you .... that new series on Channel 4 on Thursday nights?

4 She .... her parents for a new MP3 player for months!

5 He can't believe he's got tickets for the World Cup final. He .... about this for years!

6 I don't know if I like my new school yet. I .... there very long.

c Make questions to ask your partner.

1 What / favourite / group? How long / listen / …?

2 Who / favourite / author? How long / read / …?

3 What / favourite / subject? How long / study / …?

> ....> A: *What's your favourite group?*
> B: *Probably Florence and the Machine.*
> A: *How long have you been listening to them?*
> B: *For about four years.*

Interaction 2 [DVD]

Returning items to a shop

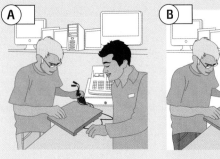

a [1.17] Listen to someone returning an item to a shop. Tick (✓) the correct picture.

b [1.17] Listen again.

1 What has the customer just bought?

2 What's the problem?

3 How long will it take to repair?

4 Is the customer happy? Why? / Why not?

c [1.17] Listen again. Who says the phrases, the shop assistant (*S*) or customer (*C*)?

1 Can I help you? | S |

2 I've just bought this. | ☐ |

3 It doesn't work properly. | ☐ |

4 What's the problem? | ☐ |

5 I've only used it once. | ☐ |

6 Do you have the receipt? | ☐ |

7 I'm sorry about that. | ☐ |

d Work with a partner.

Student A: Turn to page 118.
Student B: Turn to page 121.

Portfolio 2

A discussion essay

a Akram had to write an essay for school. The title was 'Plastic bags should be banned from my town'. Look at what he did before he started writing. Why do you think he made these notes?

> ### Intro – help environment / some towns have already banned bags
>
> **Arguments in favour**
> **Reasons to ban plastic bags. Ideas!**
>
> - Less waste
> - Less energy used to make the bags
> - Less plastic in the sea and in the countryside
> - Cleaner town
>
> **Arguments against**
> **Reasons NOT to ban plastic bags. Ideas!**
>
> - They're useful when you buy something unexpectedly.
> - No plastic bags = always carrying another bag – not cool
> - Plastic bag factories may close Lose jobs for people?
> - You can reuse plastic bags in bins at home
>
> **Conclusion – don't ban bags!**

b Read Akram's essay and tick (✓) the things he mentions from his notes above.

> ### Plastic bags should be banned from my town. Discuss.
>
> Nowadays many people are worried about the environment. Most people want to do what they can to look after our planet and some towns have been making changes to ban plastic bags.
>
> To begin with, I am going to look at the advantages of banning plastic bags. In the first place, there would be less waste and less plastic in the seas and in the countryside. Our town would be cleaner if we didn't have any plastic bags. Making bags uses a lot of energy so we would save energy too.
>
> In contrast, there are also disadvantages to consider. Plastic bags are very useful when you go to a shop unexpectedly. If we don't have plastic bags, we always have to carry another bag and sometimes that's impractical. In addition to this, the people who work in plastic bag factories could lose their jobs.
>
> To sum up, I don't think it's a good idea to ban plastic bags completely in my town. People should try to use fewer bags and only take them when they really need them, but bags shouldn't be banned completely. I've been thinking about this carefully and I believe that manufacturers should make paper bags too, so people have a choice.

c Choose one of the essay titles below and make notes with your ideas.

1 All electrical items should be repaired and reused.
2 People today produce too much waste.
3 Everyone should do something to help the environment.
4 Landfill sites should be banned. We need to find other solutions for waste.

d Write your essay. You should have four clear paragraphs:

- an introduction
- arguments in favour of the statement
- arguments against the statement
- a conclusion

e Work with a partner. Read your partner's essay. Do you share their opinion? Why? / Why not?

1

Reduce, Reuse, Recycle

The average family produces one ton of rubbish each year – about the same weight as a car. Below are some suggestions about what you can do to cut down on your waste.

Do your bit for the environment – REDUCE the amount of waste you produce now!

REDUCE REUSE RECYCLE

2

Wise up to Waste Week
12th – 19th July

Wise Up to Waste Week
Wythnos Craff am Wastraff

Think positively about waste!

What will happen to Swansea's waste in the future?

What are the alternatives to throwing things away?

How can I help tackle climate change?

Answers to these questions and many more during **'Wise up to Waste Week'**.

Waste to Wonder Workshops Create a work of art from waste.

CD, DVD, computer game and toy exchange Exchange your old CDs, DVDs, computer games and toys.

Magazine and book exchange An opportunity to swap books and magazines you have already read.

3

MILLENNIUM STADIUM

BOOK A STADIUM TOUR NOW   EVENTS   EZINE   BOOK TICKETS

HOME   EVENTS   TOURS   HOSPITALITY   TICKETS   CONFERENCES   TRAVEL INFORMATION

LATEST NEWS

Katherine Jenkins concert
Book your tickets early

RUGBY EVENTS

Wales v. England
4 February

Wales v. Ireland
12 March

4

The Great Swansea Clothes Swap

Saturday 26 July at the National Waterfront Museum

Is your wardrobe bulging with clothes you no longer wear?

Do you want to update your wardrobe without buying clothes from expensive city centre stores?

Come and take part in the Great Swansea Clothes Swap!

The Great Swansea Clothes Swap is expected to be the LARGEST clothes swap that has ever taken part in Wales. Swapping your old clothes is good for you because it helps you to replenish your wardrobe without costing you a fortune; it's good for the environment because your old clothes won't be going into landfill sites; and it's good for charity, because any items left at the end of the day will be donated to a cancer charity.

Rules:

1. Buy your ticket
Buy your ticket in advance.
Tickets £7.50, available from
www.greatswanseaclothesswap.co.uk

2. Drop off (12–5pm Saturday 26 July)
Bring at least three unwanted items of clothing to the venue.
Collect 1 token for each item you bring.
Clothes should be in good condition and wearable.
No underwear, swimwear or earrings.

3. Swap (6–8pm Saturday 26 July)
Bring your tokens and choose one item of clothing for each token.

Get ready to find your new summer wardrobe!

5

Cardiff MAS Carnival

Cardiff Bay to Civic Centre
6 Aug

FREE EVENT

It's the 22nd annual Cardiff MAS Carnival 'MAGICK: Dr Dee's World of Wonder' which brings Cardiff City Centre alive with hundreds of flamboyant costumes, carnival creations, masks, headpieces, giant puppets on backpacks and mobile sculptures.

Watch scheming magicians, cosmic spirits, shadowy demons, swashbuckling adventurers and Welsh Indian warriors as they all dance dynamically to the funky street bands through the streets of Cardiff finishing at the Admiral Big Weekend on City Hall Lawn.

The Parade
11:30am
Parade leaves Wales Millennium Centre travelling up Bute Street.
12:30pm
Along St Mary's Street where the parade stops for a half hour 'Street Jam'.
1:00pm
Continuing along The Hayes, Castle Street, Kingsway.
1:30pm
Finishing at the Admiral Cardiff Big Weekend on City Hall Lawn.

Want to join in the parade? Come along and take part in three weeks of **FREE Carnival Arts Workshops.**

For further information go to **www.swica.co.uk**

www.twitter.com/swicawales

FREE   SWICA presents: FREE

MAGICK
THE LAST ROYAL WIZARD

CARNIVAL-THEATRE SPECTACULAR
HALF HOUR FAMILY SHOW

Blysh Festival
Outside Wales Millennium Centre
Sunday 24th July 2011 at 3pm

1 Culture UK: South Wales

a Look at the information about South Wales and answer the questions.

1 What can you make in the Waste to Wonder Workshop?

2 What time and where does the Mas Carnival parade begin?

3 Who can take part in the carnival parade and what do you have to do to join in?

4 What can you do with your old books and magazines during Wise up to Waste Week?

5 Name two events you could see at the Millennium Stadium.

6 What time can you leave your clothes to swap in the Great Swansea Clothes Swap?

7 Where is the Great Swansea Clothes Swap taking place?

8 What three types of clothing and accessories are not allowed in the Great Swansea Clothes Swap?

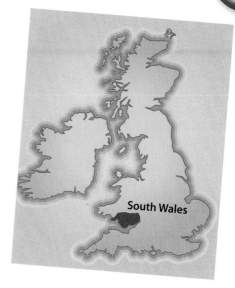

South Wales

b Complete the crossword and find a word related to the environment.

1 things we throw away (text 1)

2 swap something for something else (text 4)

3 the problems of changes to the weather caused by pollution (text 2)

4 an organisation that helps people in need (text 4)

5 try to deal with a difficult problem (text 2)

6 in good enough condition to wear (tcxt 4)

7 a large shop (text 4)

c Imagine you are going to visit South Wales. Which events would you like to take part in? Why?

2 Your project

Wise up to Waste Week in your town

a Work in a group. Make a list of ideas of some events for young people to take part in, as part of a Wise up to Waste Week in your town.

b Think about:

- What events will attract young people?
- How will it be organised?
- Where will it take place?
- How will it be advertised?
- How will it help the environment?

c Make a leaflet to advertise the 'green' event in your town.

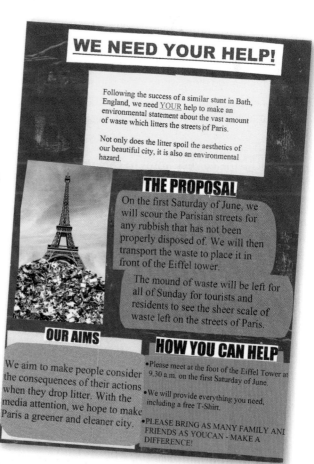

WE NEED YOUR HELP!

Following the success of a similar stunt in Bath, England, we need YOUR help to make an environmental statement about the vast amount of waste which litters the streets of Paris.

Not only does the litter spoil the aesthetics of our beautiful city, it is also an environmental hazard.

THE PROPOSAL

On the first Saturday of June, we will scour the Parisian streets for any rubbish that has not been properly disposed of. We will then transport the waste to place it in front of the Eiffel tower.

The mound of waste will be left for all of Sunday for tourists and residents to see the sheer scale of waste left on the streets of Paris.

OUR AIMS

We aim to make people consider the consequences of their actions when they drop litter. With the media attention, we hope to make Paris a greener and cleaner city.

HOW YOU CAN HELP

• Please meet at the foot of the Eiffel Tower at 9.30 a.m. on the first Saturday of June.

• We will provide everything you need, including a free T-Shirt.

• PLEASE BRING AS MANY FAMILY AND FRIENDS AS YOU CAN - MAKE A DIFFERENCE!

Review ① and ②

① Grammar

a Complete the sentences with the correct present form of the verbs.

1 Every day he .... (leave) his house at 8:45am.

2 Who .... you .... (call) now? You're always on your mobile phone!

3 They .... (wait) for the bus to arrive now.

4 I don't feel very well, I think I .... (eat) too much chocolate.

5 Frank usually .... (go) to karate lessons on Thursdays.

6 He .... (not like) getting up early.

7 How long .... you .... (live) here?

`7`

b Complete the sentences with the correct past form of the verb *do*. Use *used to* when possible.

1 What time .... you .... judo yesterday?

2 When I was younger I .... lots of activities after school but now I don't do anything.

3 .... you .... your homework last night? We have to give it in today.

4 Maria was busy when I arrived. She .... some jobs for her mum.

5 What .... you .... when I rang you last night? You didn't answer the phone.

6 He .... his homework, but he's making more effort now and he usually does it.

`6`

c (Circle) the correct words to complete the conversation.

Teacher: Have you finished the activity?

Student 1: Yes, I've ¹ *yet / just* finished it.

Student 2: No, I haven't finished ² *already / yet*. I need a few more minutes.

Teacher: OK, all the students who have ³ *yet / already* finished can turn to page 44.

Student 3: Sorry, Miss. What page?

Teacher: I've ⁴ *just / yet* told you the page. Page 44.

Student 4: And what can we do if we haven't finished ⁵ *already / yet*?

Teacher: If you haven't finished ⁶ *already / yet*, you can have five more minutes. `6`

d Write sentences. Use the present perfect continuous.

1 You / read / that book for months.

....

2 I / feel / tired since I woke up.

....

3 She / not get / any exercise recently.

....

4 He / have / problems with his motorbike all week.

....

5 How long / they / learn / to play the guitar?

....

6 What / you / do / all morning?

....

`6`

e Read the comment from a recycling message board. Choose the correct answer: A, B or C.

My camera has ¹........... broken so I ²........... it to the shop earlier today to see if they could repair it. The man ³........... that it would cost more to repair it than to buy a new one! I haven't decided what to do ⁴........... . I find it hard to believe that we can't get anything repaired these days. In the past there ⁵........... repair shops in every town, so there wasn't as much waste.

1 **A** yet   **B** already   **C** just

2 **A** took   **B** was taking   **C** didn't take

3 **A** said   **B** has said   **C** was saying

4 **A** already   **B** just   **C** yet

5 **A** was   **B** are   **C** used to be

`5`

How are you doing?

How many points have you got? Put two crosses on the chart: one for grammar and one for vocabulary.

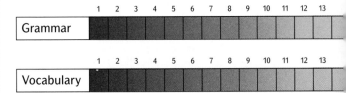

	1	2	3	4	5	6	7	8	9	10	11	12	13
Grammar													

	1	2	3	4	5	6	7	8	9	10	11	12	13
Vocabulary													

2 Vocabulary

a Complete the sentences with the words in the box.

active   energetic   fit   flexible   stretch   train
warm up   work out

1 You should .... your muscles when you've finished doing exercise.
2 I've started going to the gym because I want to get ....
3 We're going to .... for six months before we do the marathon.
4 I'm not very .... – I can't even touch my toes!
5 It isn't good to play computer games all the time – you should be more ....
6 It's important to .... properly before you start doing exercise.
7 If you want strong muscles, you should .... in the gym.
8 I just want to sit down and rest – I don't feel very .... today!

☐ 8

b Match the phrasal verbs and expressions in **bold** with the meanings.

arrive   avoid   be chosen for   be friends with
become   continue   obtain   receive

1 She was **getting** tired.
2 I must **get on with** my homework now.
3 I've just **got** a text message from Edith.
4 She hates PE and always tries to **get out of** it.
5 What time will we **get** to Paris?
6 He's trying to **get into** the football team.
7 Where can I **get** information about sports clubs?
8 I **get on with** Jack very well.

☐ 8

c Put the letters in the correct order and make words for electrical items.

1 idshwshaer ....
2 awhnsig hmcniea ....
3 acvumu ncaeelr ....
4 wicmeorva ....
5 dofo rpocessro ....
6 mubtle ryder ....
7 iarh edyrr ....
8 reefrez ....

☐ 8

d Complete the sentences with the correct form of the verbs. Add a prefix (*re-*, *over-*, *under-* or *super-*) to the verb.

charge   model   paid   priced   sleep   use

1 I always try to .... shopping bags.
2 He's so attractive – he looks like a ....!
3 Video cameras are too expensive. I think they're ....!
4 Some young people do jobs that are ...., so they earn very little money.
5 I can't phone my friends because I need to .... my phone.
6 I need to get to bed early – I don't want to .... tomorrow.

☐ 6

Correct it!

Correct these typical learner errors from Units 1 and 2.

1 I hope I will get in university next year.
....
2 He's always having breakfast every day at 8 o'clock.
....
3 She's totally agreeing with her parents.
....
4 Thanks for explaining that. I'm understanding now.
....
5 You can use a hairdryer for dry your hair.
....
6 I need a new food procesor.
....
7 We've finished just our lesson.
....
8 He's gone to London four times.
....
9 We've lived in this house since three months.
....
10 She's studying English for five years.
....

GREEN: Great! Tell your teacher your score!
YELLOW: Not bad, but go to the website for extra practice.
RED: Talk to your teacher and look at Units 1 and 2 again. Go to the website for extra practice.

14	15	16	17	18	19	20	21	22	23	24	25	26	27	28	29	30

14	15	16	17	18	19	20	21	22	23	24	25	26	27	28	29	30

3 Forces of nature

will and *going to*
Future continuous
Vocabulary: Natural disasters; Outdoor equipment
Interaction 3: Getting ready for a trip

(A) **The eye of the storm**

(B) **Blazing inferno**

(C) **Water, water everywhere**

1 Read and listen

a Read the texts quickly and match them with the titles A–C.

1 ☐ *Naima, 17, India*

Right now I'm in our flat in Delhi. There are dark, heavy monsoon clouds, so it's going to rain soon, very hard and for a long time. Tomorrow my father is going to make sure all our windows are secure so they will keep the rain out. We're also going to buy extra food and drinking water – we expect it will be difficult to get to the shops once the rain starts, but I think we'll cope with the situation if we prepare for it. In the city there are often floods and the electricity sometimes gets cut off. But that's nothing compared to what can happen in the countryside. Every year there are huge floods near rivers or the sea, and hundreds of people lose their homes.

2 ☐ *Jon, 16, USA*

I live in the state of Mississippi. It's part of 'Tornado Alley', an area which has a lot of tornadoes, or 'twisters', every spring. About 1,000 tornadoes occur in different parts of the USA every year. This year we had a really bad storm. A huge twister, 1.6 km wide, came right through the centre of town with winds blowing at about 240 km per hour. Like most tornadoes, it only lasted for about 10 minutes, but lots of buildings were damaged and people got hurt very badly. We were lucky, though, because our house wasn't touched. Most people think our town will probably be OK next year, because it isn't very likely that a tornado will hit it two years in a row. But we're going to make our basement stronger, just in case.

3 ☐ *Brittany, 18, Australia*

In Victoria we often get heat waves in January and February, when temperatures can sometimes be as high as 44°C. Heat waves increase the risk of forest fires, or bushfires. We've just had a few bushfires in my area. Luckily, nobody was badly hurt this time, but hundreds of houses were burnt to the ground. The fires reached very high temperatures and a lot of animals, like kangaroos and cows, were killed. Lots of people volunteered to help as firefighters, but I'm helping to look after the people who have lost their homes. We've got a place for them to stay and we're making them food, but maybe the most important thing is to talk to them and listen to them. They're in shock because they've just lost everything they had.

b 🔊 **1.18** Read the texts again and listen. Then answer the questions.

1 How is Naima's family preparing for the monsoon?
2 What are the effects of the monsoon?
3 Where is 'Tornado Alley'?
4 How big was the tornado that went through Jon's town?
5 What are the effects of the bushfires?
6 What is Brittany doing at the moment?

c Work in a group. Answer the questions.

1 Do you know about any natural disasters?
2 What do people do to prepare for extreme weather in your country?
3 Would you volunteer to help in an emergency? Why? / Why not?

2 Vocabulary Natural disasters

a 🔊 **1.19** Match the pictures with the words for natural disasters. Then listen and check.

> **1** avalanche **2** drought **3** earthquake
> **4** flood **5** heat wave **6** hurricane
> **7** tsunami **8** volcanic eruption

A

B

C

D

E

F

G

H

b Choose the correct words.

1 Two skiers died in the *avalanche / drought*.
2 If it continues to rain, there might be a *heat wave / flood* in the town.
3 The *drought / tsunami* has continued for three months now, and a lot of plants have died.
4 A *heat wave / hurricane* has the power to destroy trees and buildings.

c 🔊 **1.20** Listen to the conversations and weather reports. Which of the things in Exercise 2a are the people talking about?

1 ....
2 ....
3 ....
4 ....
5 ....

d Work with a partner. Answer the questions.

1 What types of weather do you think are more difficult to live with? Why?
2 What's the worst weather you have experienced? What happened?

3 Pronunciation DVD

/uː/ and /ʊ/

a 🔊 **1.21** Sometimes the same combination of letters can be pronounced differently. Listen to these words.

| /uː/ | monsoon | boot | food |
| /ʊ/ | look | foot | good |

b 🔊 **1.22** Listen to the pronunciation of the underlined words and tick (✓) the correct column.

	/uː/	/ʊ/
1 He bought a <u>book</u> about hurricanes.		
2 It'll stop raining <u>soon</u>.		
3 I'm going to <u>school</u> in half an hour.		
4 It's a clear night. Can you see the <u>moon</u>?		
5 The earth <u>shook</u> for about three minutes.		
6 The lightning struck somewhere in the <u>wood</u>.		

c 🔊 **1.22** Listen again and repeat.

d 🔊 **1.23** Listen and repeat.

> *Look at the rain! It's good that the monsoon will finish soon!*

Culture Vulture

Did you know that between 2000 and 2010 Britain had seven serious floods, two tornadoes, two heat waves, two periods of heavy snow and one hurricane? Does your country often have extreme weather?

4 Grammar

will and going to

a Look at the examples and match them with the uses.

1 *There are dark, heavy monsoon clouds, so it's **going to rain** soon.*
2 *We expect it **will be** difficult to get to the shops once the rain starts.*
3 *But we're **going to make** our basement stronger, just in case.*
4 *I'll **help** you!*

A a decision made at the time of speaking (sometimes an offer or promise)
B a future plan or intention
C a prediction based on present evidence
D a prediction about the future (often with *think, hope, expect,* etc.)

Grammar reference: Workbook page 82

b Complete the sentences with *will* or *going to* and the verbs in brackets.

1 I've made a homework plan. I
.............................(write) my history essay tomorrow.
2 Do you think there ....(be) more extreme weather in the future?
3 A: This bag is really heavy!
   B: I ....(carry) it for you!
4 Look out! You ....(fall)!
5 I ....(not tidy) my room this evening. I want to go out.
6 I expect you ....(have) a great time on holiday.

Check it out!

- We use the present continuous and *going to* for future arrangements.
  I'm meeting / going to meet my friends later.
- However, we can't use the present continuous for intentions, if there isn't an arrangement.
  One day I'**m going to buy** a big car.
  NOT ~~One day I'm buying a big car.~~

c 🔊 1.24 Circle the correct words, then listen and check your answers.

Have you heard [1] *what's happening / what will happen* at school next Friday? [2] *We'll have / We're having* a special Mad Hair Day to raise money for people who are homeless after the earthquake. If you pay £1, you can come to school with a crazy hairstyle or a silly hat. [3] *It'll be / It's being* fun! Sam and I [4] *are going to spray / will spray* our hair different colours. [5] *We're going / We'll go* to a concert after school. [6] *It's being / It'll be* good to have funky hair.

d Work with a partner. Complete the sentences so they are true for you, then compare.

1 After class, I think …
2 This evening I …
3 At the weekend I …
4 Next year, I …

5 Speak

a Work on your own. You are going to volunteer after a natural disaster. Think of a disaster and fill in the information.

Country: ....
Disaster: ....
Problems: ....
....
....
....
Your job: ....

b Work with a partner. Take turns to interview each other about your volunteer work. Ask about the country, the disaster, the problems and your partner's job. Make notes.

c Compare your notes. Which volunteer's job will be more difficult? Why?

(6) Vocabulary

Outdoor equipment

a ◁»)) **1.25** Match the words with the pictures.
Then listen and check.

1 anorak 2 fleece 3 goggles 4 insect repellent
5 rucksack 6 sleeping bag 7 sun cream
8 torch 9 walking boots 10 wetsuit

b Complete the sentences with words from
Exercise 6a.

1 My .... is really comfortable to carry,
even when it's heavy.

2 He wears a .... to keep warm when
he goes windsurfing.

3 When we go camping we sleep in a
....

4 She's got very pale skin so she takes lots of
.... when she travels to hot countries.

5 I always get bitten by mosquitoes when I forget to
take ....

6 They forgot to take a .... with them
so they couldn't see anything at night.

7 He always takes a .... when he goes
climbing. It's lighter and warmer than a normal
jumper.

8 Her T-shirt was dry because she was wearing an
.... over it, but her jeans got very wet
in the rain.

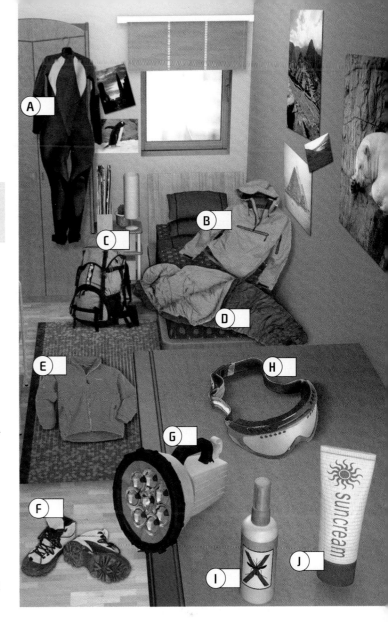

c Imagine you are going on these trips. Write three items from Exercise 6a that you would take with you.

Surfing	Skiing	Camping	Trekking	Safari
			fleece walking boots rucksack	

(7) Listen

a ◁»)) **1.26** Listen to three conversations about
people getting ready to go on holiday. Number
the items in the order you hear them.

skis ☐   goggles ☐

sleeping bag ☐   snowboard ☐

sun cream ☐   walking boots ☐

insect repellent ☐   fleece ☐

b ◁»)) **1.26** Listen again. Are the sentences *right*
(✓) or *wrong* (✗)? Correct the wrong sentences.

1 Dan and Ben both need a new sleeping bag.

2 Dan and Ben will have to take fleeces on
their trip.

3 Jess and Simone are going to share a bottle
of insect repellent.

4 Jess and Simone are going to the beach on
Thursday.

5 Toby is really good at snowboarding.

6 Marlene and Toby are both going to go
snowboarding.

c Work with a partner. Which of the holidays
would you like to go on? Why?

8 Grammar

Future continuous

a Look at the examples. Then (circle) the correct words to complete the rules.

> ···→ *Next Friday we'll be sunbathing and swimming in the sea.*
> *We won't be sleeping in a tent.*

- We use the future continuous for actions in progress at **a** / **no** specific time in the future.
- We form the future continuous with *will be +* **infinitive** / **verb + -ing**

Grammar reference: Workbook page 84

b Complete the sentences with the verbs in brackets. Use the future continuous or *will*.

1 That cheap sun cream isn't waterproof. I .... (get) this one instead.
2 This time next week we .... (walk) in the Himalayas. I can't believe it.
3 I think perhaps I .... (get) a job in the campsite shop again this summer.
4 Just think, in three days' time you .... (lie) on a sunny beach.
5 Call me at seven o'clock. I .... (not do) my homework at that time.

c Work in a group. Ask and answer questions about the future. Add extra words if necessary.

in the summer   at 9am on Saturday
this time next Thursday   in 10 years' time

A: *What will you be doing in the summer?*
B: *I'll be working at the café in town.*

Interaction 3 DVD

Getting ready for a trip

a ◀))) 1.27 Listen to Jack and Millie deciding what to take on a camping trip. Tick (✓) the things in the picture that they are definitely going to take.

b ◀))) 1.27 Listen again and match the sentence halves.

1 We'll definitely need	**A** be easy to buy food.
2 I reckon it'll	**B** just in case.
3 Let's take the tin opener,	**C** we'll need the jumpers.
4 We'll decide on	**D** take the fleeces?
5 Do you think it'll	**E** be cold in the evening?
6 Shall we	**F** sleeping bags.
7 I don't think	**G** the stove later.

c Work with a partner.

Student A: Turn to page 118.
Student B: Turn to page 121.

Portfolio 3

An email asking for information

a Jez has seen this advert online. Read the advert. What three types of work does it advertise?

Adventure volunteer programmes for teens

Doing voluntary work is an exciting and rewarding way to travel to other countries. Make a positive contribution to the places you visit by helping others. At 'Reach Out' we organise volunteer trips for young people aged 16–18. If you are simply looking for a fantastic adventure, we also offer great trips packed with action, supervised by experts.

Wildlife conservation in Zimbabwe

House building in Thailand

Help children improve their survival skills in the Canadian mountains

Write to us with your questions and we will send you detailed information.

b Read Jez's email. Which trip does he choose and why? What does he want to know?

c Read Jez's email again. Find and correct six spelling mistakes.

d You have seen these trips advertised on a website. Choose the trip you would prefer to go on.

1 **Look after cute monkeys in Sri Lanka!**
2 **Tree planting and flora conservation in Costa Rica.**
3 **Teach sports, art or basic computer skills to children in Tanzania.**

e Write an email to explain which trip you want to go on and to ask for more information. Ask about some of the things in the box. Check your spelling.

> getting to and from the destination
> the length of the trip   clothes   equipment
> activities during the trip   places to stay
> food   weather   other information

f Work with a partner. Read your partner's email. Which trip does he/she choose and why? Does he/she ask good questions?

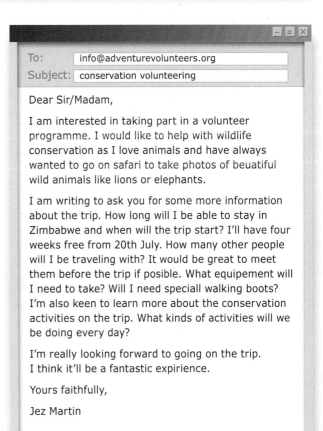

To: info@adventurevolunteers.org
Subject: conservation volunteering

Dear Sir/Madam,

I am interested in taking part in a volunteer programme. I would like to help with wildlife conservation as I love animals and have always wanted to go on safari to take photos of beuatiful wild animals like lions or elephants.

I am writing to ask you for some more information about the trip. How long will I be able to stay in Zimbabwe and when will the trip start? I'll have four weeks free from 20th July. How many other people will I be traveling with? It would be great to meet them before the trip if posible. What equipement will I need to take? Will I need speciall walking boots? I'm also keen to learn more about the conservation activities on the trip. What kinds of activities will we be doing every day?

I'm really looking forward to going on the trip. I think it'll be a fantastic expirience.

Yours faithfully,

Jez Martin

File Edit View Insert Format Tools Actions Help

http://interactive.cambridge.org/

Arctic Action

1 Can you imagine trying to survive in freezing cold Arctic weather? Weather conditions have always been extreme in this area but, because of climate change, the Arctic is in danger. Sea temperatures are rising, the ice is melting and the ecosystem is changing dramatically. Many people are campaigning to protect the Arctic and we found out about three campaigns that are really making an impact.

THE ARCTIC — FACTS AND FIGURES

- The Arctic covers more than one sixth of the Earth's surface.
- The Arctic includes the Arctic Ocean and parts of Canada, Greenland (part of Denmark), Russia, the United States (Alaska), Iceland, Norway, Sweden and Finland
- The Arctic Ocean is the smallest ocean on the planet.
- The lowest temperature recorded in the Arctic is −68°C.
- The North Pole is on sea ice that floats on the Arctic Ocean.

2 STUDENTS ON ICE

Students on Ice offers unique educational expeditions to the Arctic and Antarctic for young people aged 14–18. This Canadian organisation brings teachers and scientists together to work with students from around the world who are interested in learning about the polar regions. They travel on a ship and make trips onto the land and ice to learn about local communities, wildlife, and marine and plant life. Learning about these places in a classroom is one thing, but learning about them when you are physically there is completely different! The founder of the organisation, Geoff Green, hopes that when participants return home they will be Polar Ambassadors. This means they will be able to give talks, do research and motivate others to become interested in protecting the polar regions.

3 National Inuit Youth Council

The **National Inuit Youth Council** (NIYC) works to protect the interests of young Inuit people, who are natives of the Arctic region. The organisation campaigns to preserve their language and culture. These young people know that climate change will directly affect them and they need to be heard. This group is also trying to find out more about climate change. One group of young people met in Inuvik, northern Canada, to take part in a conference on climate change. The participants had the opportunity to learn from experts. As well as learning about climate change in talks and presentations, they also went out on 'field trips' to learn more about the land and to experiment with new green technologies such as solar-powered cars. They all agreed that it is important to campaign to help slow down the climate changes that are affecting the landscape and will affect the whole planet in the future.

4 World Wide Fund for Nature (WWF) Polar Bear Tracker

The **World Wide Fund for Nature** (WWF) is working hard to try and save the polar bear, whose habitat is threatened because of global warming. They have launched the Polar Bear Tracker campaign to help people understand why polar bears are in danger and to get people involved in following their progress. They have put special electronic tags on six polar bears in Canada's Hudson Bay. Have a look below to see how the WWF team managed to tag these enormous creatures. The electronic tags receive satellite signals and anybody who is interested can track the polar bears' movements live online.

1 Culture World: The Arctic

a Read the webzine quickly and choose the best title for the page.

1 Arctic animals in danger
2 Working to save the Arctic
3 The history and people of the Arctic
4 Young people studying the Arctic

b Read the texts again and answer the questions.

1 Why is the Arctic in danger?
2 What can students learn on the *Students on Ice* programme?
3 Where is the organisation *Students on Ice* from?
4 What does the NIYC want to save?
5 Why is the polar bear's habitat in danger?
6 Who can track the polar bears?

c Find the words in the texts that mean …

1 changing from a solid to a liquid because of heat (text 1)
2 a powerful effect that something has on a situation or a person (text 1)
3 an organised journey, especially a long one for a particular purpose (text 2)
4 an event where there are talks about a particular subject (text 3)
5 visits made by students to study something away from their school or college (text 3)
6 follow a person or animal by using electronic equipment (text 4).

d Work with a partner. Answer the questions.

1 Would you like to go on an expedition to the Arctic? Why? / Why not?
2 What do you think about the Polar Bear Tracker campaign? Do you think it would be interesting to follow a polar bear? Why? / Why not?
3 Do you think that politicians and world leaders really listen to young people's opinions? Why? / Why not?

2 Your project

Campaigning for action

a Work in a group. Complete a table like the one below with information about a campaign you would like to begin in your area.

Campaign	Location	Problem	Action
WWF's Polar Bear Tracker Campaign.	Hudson Bay, Canada.	Polar bears are in danger as their habitat is changing.	Tag and track a group of polar bears so that people around the world can follow them.

b Plan your campaign. Think about events you can organise, and different ways you can advertise your campaign.

c Make a poster or flyer to advertise your campaign. Include pictures, and details of the events you have planned.

4 Friends 4ever

if, when, as soon as and *unless*
First and second conditional review
Vocabulary: Friendship; Adjectives of personality
Interaction 4: Giving and receiving advice

1 Vocabulary

Friendship

a 🔊 **1.28** Read the text and match the words in bold with the definitions. Listen and check.

Jack and I are best mates. We've known each other since we were five. We usually [1]**get on well**, but the other day he really [2]**let** me **down**. I know it's stupid to [3]**fall out with** each other over something so silly but I [4]**was** really **cross with** him after what he did. He borrowed my phone without asking and sent a stupid text to our mate Leon, pretending he was me! It was supposed to be a joke but I didn't think it was very funny and we [5]**had a** huge **argument**. He often plays jokes on people but usually I never [6]**tell on** him. When he gets in trouble, I always [7]**stick up for** him – but this time he went too far. I guess in a few days we'll [8]**make up with** each other and be friends again but for now, we're not talking.

A become friendly with someone again after arguing with them

B make someone feel disappointed with you

C like and be friendly to each other

D speak angrily with someone because you disagree with them

E tell someone about something bad that someone else has done

F stop being friendly with someone

G be annoyed or angry with someone

H defend or support a person

b Put the expressions in Exercise 1a into the word webs.

tell on

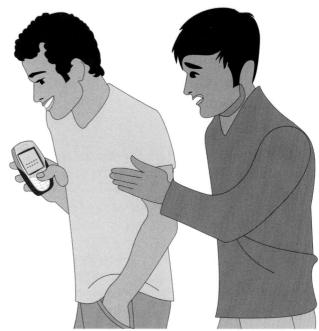

c Do you know any more words or expressions to do with friendship? Write them down.

d Work with a partner. Complete the sentences so they are true for you, then compare.

1 My ideal best mate is …
2 The last time I had an argument was …
3 The last time a friend let me down was …

2 Pronunciation 🅓🅥🅓

Friendly intonation

a 🔊 **1.29** Listen to the speakers and decide if they sound friendly or unfriendly. Write *A* or *B* in the correct column.

	Friendly	Unfriendly
1 I'll call you later. Bye!	*A*	*B*
2 Have you got time for a chat?		
3 That video isn't bad.		
4 I really don't have time to talk now.		

b 🔊 **1.29** Listen again, check and practise saying the sentences in a friendly way.

③ Read and listen

a Read the text quickly and choose the best title.

1 Mixing work and friendship doesn't work
2 Best mates … but only online
3 An unusual way to find your best friend … and a job

Charlie McDonnell and Alex Day are friends. They got to know each other on YouTube and they soon realised that they had a few things in common. They both love making videos, and they both write and sing their own songs. They are both huge fans of the science-fiction TV series Doctor Who and they have a similar sense of humour. In fact, they have so many things in common and get on so well with each other that they even live and work together. They do occasionally argue and fall out with each other over something really silly, but they always make up soon afterwards. In many ways, Charlie and Alex are just like most young flatmates, but their shared hobbies have turned into a career for both of them.

Charlie had been making video blogs on YouTube for just a couple of months when he became an online celebrity almost overnight. YouTube decided to put his video called 'How to get featured on YouTube' on their homepage and the number of views increased from 150 to over 4,000! Now he has had more than 40 million views. He has already appeared on numerous TV shows and he has given presentations at Google conferences. As soon as you see Charlie in action, you'll agree with his viewers that he's a great entertainer.

Alex, known online as Nerimon, is a successful musician and since he started making videos on YouTube he has become an online celebrity. His latest project is a band called Sons of Admirals, which is made up of Charlie,

Eddplant and Tom Milsom, all fellow bloggers. Between them they have had over 67 million video views, so they already reach a very large audience. If this continues, the band will be a huge success.

Watching their videos, it's clear that Charlie and Alex share a mutual respect. They often help each other out by promoting their friend's content on their own sites. Charlie was recently asked to present an award at the BAFTAs, which is the British Academy of Film and Television Arts. Who did he invite as a guest? Yes, you've guessed it, not his mum or a girlfriend, but Alex, who blogged about it the next day! Unless something strange happens, Charlie and Alex will continue to enjoy their success, and their friendship. Will they still be the best of friends when one of them becomes really famous? Only time will tell.

b ◀))) 1.30 Read the text again and listen. Write *C* (Charlie), *A* (Alex) or *B* (both Charlie and Alex).

1 One of his first videos got onto the YouTube homepage. ....
2 He's been on television programmes. ....
3 His online name is Nerimon. ....
4 He's given presentations at conferences. ....
5 He's in the band The Sons of Admirals. ....
6 He respects his best friend. ....
7 He presented an important award. ....
8 He blogged about an award ceremony. ....

c Work in a group. Answer the questions.

1 Have you ever got to know someone on the internet? How?
2 Do you read blogs or watch videos? Which ones?
3 Have you ever made a video and put it on the internet? If so, tell your group about it.
4 Would you like to make a career out of your hobbies? Why? / Why not?

(4) Grammar

if, when, as soon as and *unless*

a Look at the examples. Then (circle) the correct words to complete the rules.

> ⤷ ***As soon as*** *you see Charlie in action, you'll agree that he's a great entertainer.*
>
> ***If*** *this continues, the band will be a huge success.*
>
> ***Unless*** *something strange happens, Charlie and Alex will continue to enjoy their success.*
>
> *Will they still be the best of friends* ***when*** *one of them becomes really famous?*

We use:

- **when** / **as soon as** to mean 'immediately when'.
- **unless** / **when** to mean 'if not'.
- *when* for situations that we **are** / **aren't** sure will happen.
- *if* for situations that we **are** / **aren't** sure will happen.
- *if, when, as soon as* and *unless* with **the present simple** / **will**.

Grammar reference: Workbook page 84

Check it out!

- We use *unless* to make part of a conditional sentence negative.
  Unless I study more, I'll fail the course =
  If I don't study more, I'll fail the course.
- We use *unless* + positive verb.
  Unless I leave now, I'll miss the bus.
  NOT ~~Unless I don't leave now, I'll miss the bus~~.

b Complete the second sentence so it has the same meaning as the first.

1 I'll only buy the dress if I have enough money.
   I won't buy the dress .... I have enough money.

2 Unless you help me with my homework, I won't go out this evening.
   If .... with my homework, I won't go out this evening.

3 We won't get tickets if we don't buy them today.
   We won't get tickets unless .... today.

4 Unless the bus comes soon, we'll miss the beginning of the film.
   If the bus .... , we'll miss the beginning of the film.

c Work with a partner. Answer the questions.

1 What will you do as soon as this class finishes?
2 What will you do when you get home today?

(5) Listen

a Work with a partner. Answer the questions.

1 When do you usually see your friends?
2 What things do you do together?

b 🔊 **1.31** Listen to three people talking about friends. Match the speakers with the photos. Write *D* (Dan), *H* (Helen) or *M* (Molly).

A

B

C

c 🔊 **1.31** Listen again. Are the sentences *right* (✓) or *wrong* (✗)?

1 Helen usually gets on very well with her best friend.
2 Helen waited for a long time at the cinema.
3 Dan's friend supports the same football team as him.
4 Dan sees his friend every week.
5 Molly has met her friend a few times.
6 Molly often talks to her friend by phone.

Culture Vulture

Did you know that the average teenager in the USA has 75 friends on their social networking site and 32 friends on their mobile phones? Do you think online friends are as good as real friends? Why / Why not?

6 Vocabulary

Adjectives of personality

a 🔊 **1.32** Match the sentences. Then listen and check.

1 He talks non-stop.
2 Callum always does lots of housework for his grandmother.
3 One minute she's happy and the next she's sad.
4 I always have a great time with Jack.
5 Chloe listens to other people's problems and really understands how they feel.
6 He's so relaxed and doesn't usually get cross with anyone.
7 She's funny, but she doesn't always show respect.
8 Suzy always says 'please' and 'thank you'.
9 I can't believe he shouts at his parents.
10 She's friendly, energetic and likes meeting new people.

A She's a bit **cheeky**.
B She's always **sympathetic**.
C He's so **rude**!
D He's really **chatty**.
E He's the most **laid-back** person I know.
F He's **fun** to be with.
G She's so **moody**.
H He's really **helpful**.
I She's so **polite**.
J She's really **outgoing**.

b Write the adjectives from Exercise 6a in the circles according to their meaning.

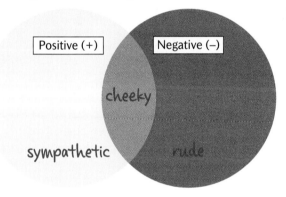

Positive (+)   Negative (–)

cheeky

sympathetic   rude

> ### Check it out!
>
> ● *Fun* = entertaining and enjoyable.
> *Funny* = making you smile or laugh.
> The new theme park is really **fun**.
> NOT ~~The new theme park is really funny~~.

c Do you know any more adjectives of personality? Add them to the circles in Exercise 6b.

d Complete the sentences with the adjectives in Exercise 6a.

1 She's really .... She never stops talking!
2 You never know if he's going to be happy or sad – he's really .... these days.
3 We always have a good time together – he's ....
4 Both my parents are quite .... They don't worry much and they don't usually get stressed.
5 Jack works as a volunteer in a youth club. He does loads of work for the club – he's really ....
6 I gave him a birthday present and he never thanked me – he's so ....

e Think of four adjectives to describe each of these people. Then compare your ideas with a partner.

> you   your best friend   a family member
> your favourite actor or singer

7 Speak

Work with a partner. Ask and answer the questions. Explain your answers using adjectives from Exercise 6a.

Who would you choose to …

1 ask for help with a difficult problem?
2 tell a secret to?
3 take with you to a party?
4 go shopping with?
5 go on holiday with?

A: *Who would you ask for help with a difficult problem?*
B: *My best friend, Richard. He's always sympathetic when I have a problem. And you?*
A: *My older sister Anya. She's always helpful.*

(8) Grammar

First and second conditional review

a Look at the examples. Which are the first conditional and which are the second conditional?

> 1 **If I go** to the match next Saturday, **I'll see** him there.
> 2 **If she phones** me tonight, **I won't answer** my phone.
> 3 **How would** you feel **if** your best mate totally **forgot** you?

Circle the correct words to complete the rules.

- We use the **first** / **second** conditional for possible future situations.
- We use the **first** / **second** conditional for imaginary situations or situations that are impossible or very unlikely.
- We form the first conditional with *If* + **present** / **past** simple + *will/won't* + infinitive without *to*.
- We form the second conditional with *If* + **present** / **past** simple + *would(n't)* + infinitive without *to*.
- The *if* clause **has to** / **doesn't have to** come first in the sentence.

Grammar reference: Workbook page 86

b Write sentences in the first or second conditional.

1 she / finish her essay tomorrow / go to the beach
2 he / meet a really famous singer / tell all his friends
3 they / be unhappy / it / rain / at the music festival / next weekend
4 we / miss the plane / traffic / not move soon
5 you / go to study / in the USA / you / keep in touch with your friends
6 she / buy / a new car / she win the lottery

Check it out!

- We never use *if* + *would* in the same clause in conditional sentences.
  If we made up, I'd be happy.
  NOT ~~If we would make up, I'd be happy.~~

c Work in small groups. Answer the questions.

1 What would you do if you saw your favourite actor in the street?
2 If you have some free time this evening, what will you do?
3 If you fell out with a good friend, what would you do?
4 If you could live in any country in the world, where would you live? Why?

Interaction 4

Giving and receiving advice

a 🔊 1.33 Listen to the conversation. What's Oliver worried about?

b 🔊 1.33 Listen again. Number the expressions in the order you hear them.

A What do you think I should do? ☐
B If I were you, I'd … ☐
C I'm not sure about that. ☐
D I'm (a bit) worried about … ☐
E Maybe you're right. ☐

c Write the phrases in Exercise b in the correct columns.

1 Asking for advice	2 Giving advice
Have you got a minute?	Why don't you *talk to him*?
What would you do?	How about … (*-ing*)?
....	....

3 Accepting advice	4 Rejecting advice
Yeah, I guess you're right.	I don't think that's the answer.
....	....

d Work with a partner.
Student A: Turn to page 118.
Student B: Turn to page 121.

Portfolio 4

An informal email to a friend

a Emma and Laura are online friends who often chat and write emails to each other, especially when they have a problem. Read the first two messages and then answer the questions.

1 What's Laura's problem?
2 Does Emma give good advice?
3 What would you do if you were Laura?

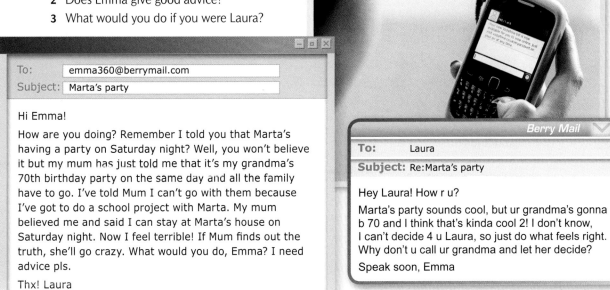

To: emma360@berrymail.com
Subject: Marta's party

Hi Emma!

How are you doing? Remember I told you that Marta's having a party on Saturday night? Well, you won't believe it but my mum has just told me that it's my grandma's 70th birthday party on the same day and all the family have to go. I've told Mum I can't go with them because I've got to do a school project with Marta. My mum believed me and said I can stay at Marta's house on Saturday night. Now I feel terrible! If Mum finds out the truth, she'll go crazy. What would you do, Emma? I need advice pls.

Thx! Laura

Berry Mail

To: Laura
Subject: Re:Marta's party

Hey Laura! How r u?

Marta's party sounds cool, but ur grandma's gonna b 70 and I think that's kinda cool 2! I don't know, I can't decide 4 u Laura, so just do what feels right. Why don't u call ur grandma and let her decide?

Speak soon, Emma

b Now read the next two messages.

1 Did Laura take Emma's advice?
2 Did Laura's grandmother react as you expected?

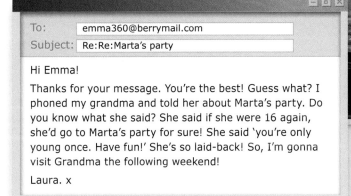

To: emma360@berrymail.com
Subject: Re:Re:Marta's party

Hi Emma!

Thanks for your message. You're the best! Guess what? I phoned my grandma and told her about Marta's party. Do you know what she said? She said if she were 16 again, she'd go to Marta's party for sure! She said 'you're only young once. Have fun!' She's so laid-back! So, I'm gonna visit Grandma the following weekend!

Laura. x

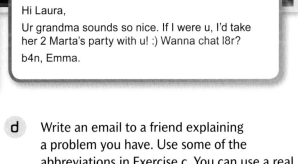

Berry Mail

To: Laura
Subject: Re:Re:Re:Marta's party

Hi Laura,
Ur grandma sounds so nice. If I were u, I'd take her 2 Marta's party with u! :) Wanna chat l8r?
b4n, Emma.

c Abbreviations and informal phrases are sometimes used in informal emails. Write the meanings. Use the messages to help you.

1 b4n   Bye for now   8 kinda ....
2 gonna ....   9 2 ....
3 wanna ....   10 b ....
4 4 ....   11 ur ....
5 u ....   12 thx ....
6 r ....   13 pls ....
7 l8r ....   14 x ....

d Write an email to a friend explaining a problem you have. Use some of the abbreviations in Exercise c. You can use a real problem or choose one of these:

1 You have fallen out with your best friend.
2 You're not getting on very well with someone in your family.
3 You borrowed something important from a friend and have lost it.

e Work with a partner. Read your partner's email. What advice would you give them?

Friendship Train

1 Song

a 🔊 **1.34** Listen to the first verse of the song. What do you think the main idea is?

- war is terrible
- the world is being destroyed
- people should try to get on with each other
- people are all different

b 🔊 **1.34** Listen again and ⟨circle⟩ the correct word.

Calling out to everyone across the nation

Said the world today is in a *desperate / terrible* situation

Listen now, stealing, burning, fighting, killing, nothing but *corruption / abduction*

It looks like mankind is on the eve of *discovery / destruction*

People, let me tell you that

We've got to learn to *be / live* with each other

No matter what race, creed or *colour / language*

I just got to tell you what the world needs now is love and *understanding / comprehension*

So get on board the friendship train

Everybody shake my hand, *make / meet* a friend now.

c 🔊 **1.35** Match the parts of the sentences from the next verse of the song. Then listen and check.

1 We've got to start today
2 We can do it, I can prove it, but
3 So get on board
4 Everybody,

A shake my hand, shake a hand
B only if our hearts are willing
C the friendship train
D to make tomorrow a brighter day for our children

d 🔊 **1.36** Put the words from the last part of the song in order. Then listen and check.

1 train / stands / This / justice / for
2 freedom / This / for / train / stands
3 for / harmony / train / and / This / peace / stands
4 love, love, love / for / on / stands / train / so / come / This

Check it out!

- In colloquial US English, *don't* is often used for *doesn't*.
  It **don't** matter what you look like.

e 🔊 **1.37** Listen to the song again. Then work in a group. Do you agree with the opinions in the song? Why? / Why not?

1 The world today is full of violence and corruption.
2 Everybody should get on with everybody else, no matter what nationality, religion or colour they are.
3 It doesn't matter what you look like if you are a good person.

② Sound check

a 🔊 **1.38** Listen to the first two lines of the song. All the stressed syllables are <u>underlined</u>.

<u>Call</u>ing <u>out</u> to <u>e</u>veryone a<u>cross</u> the <u>na</u>tion
Said the <u>world</u> to<u>day</u> is in a <u>des</u>perate situ<u>a</u>tion

b 🔊 **1.39** Listen to these lines and <u>underline</u> all the stressed syllables.

It don't matter what you look like, people,
Or who you are
If your heart is in the right place
Talking about the right place
You're welcome aboard

c 🔊 **1.39** Listen again and say the lines at the same time as the recording.

The Temptations

③ Musical notes

The 1970s

a 🔊 **1.40** Listen to some different types of music from the 1970s. Number the pictures in the order you hear them.

Disco

Punk

Reggae

THE 1970s

The song *Friendship Train* is by an American band called The Temptations. They were a male group formed in 1960 by the Motown record label, and they were one of the most successful soul/funk groups in musical history, selling tens of millions of albums.

At that time, other musical styles were also popular, including disco, punk and reggae. These musical styles were all very different from each other, and they each had their own distinctive hairstyles and fashions.

b Which of the 1970s music and fashion styles do you like best? Why?

Review 3 and 4

1 Grammar

a Complete the sentences with the verbs in brackets and the correct form of *will* or *going to*.

1 Next Saturday Jack _____ (go) shopping with his mum.

2 That suitcase looks really heavy, I _____ (help) you if you want.

3 I promise I _____ (not tell) anybody!

4 What _____ (do) tomorrow if it's raining?

5 If you're not back by 11 o'clock I _____ (send) you a text to see if you're OK.

6 I always know when my computer _____ (crash) because it makes a strange noise.

7 I don't think I _____ (pass) the exam.

☐ 7

b Imagine you and your friends are going on an adventure holiday next week. This is the holiday plan. Complete the sentences with the future continuous.

	Morning	Afternoon
Monday	arrive at the camp	walk in the mountains
Tuesday	swim in the lake	rest
Wednesday	bungee jumping	trek in the jungle
Thursday	learn rock climbing	mountain biking

1 On Monday at 4pm we _____ in the mountains.

2 On Tuesday morning we _____ in the lake.

3 On Tuesday afternoon we _____ .

4 On Wednesday morning we _____ doing our homework.

5 We _____ in the jungle on Wednesday afternoon.

6 We _____ rock climbing on Thursday morning.

☐ 6

c Circle the correct words.

1 We'll play tennis later *unless / as soon as* it rains.

2 I'll call you later *if / unless* I have enough time.

3 We should buy tickets *if / as soon as* they go on sale, to get good seats.

4 I'll be famous all over the world *if / when* I win this competition!

5 We'll be late *if / unless* we don't leave soon!

6 I'm sure Jack will be at the party *as soon as / unless* he's ill.

☐ 6

d Complete the sentences with *will*, *won't*, *would* or *wouldn't*.

1 If Billy didn't have to go to school today, he _____ stay at home and play video games.

2 What _____ you do if you found a wallet on the floor?

3 You _____ arrive too early if you leave now. Wait a few minutes.

4 If your mum has time, she _____ help you with your homework when she gets home.

5 He _____ study English if it wasn't compulsory.

6 If she read one page a day, she _____ finish the book by the end of the year. ☐ 6

e Complete the second sentence so that it means the same as the first.

1 Phone me the moment you arrive.
Phone me as soon _____ .

2 I won't buy a computer if I don't get the job.
I won't buy a computer unless _____ .

3 I'll go travelling for six months unless I get a job.
If I get a job, _____ .

4 My plan is to do all my homework tonight.
I'm _____ .

5 The tickets went on sale and she bought one immediately.
She bought a ticket as _____ .

☐ 5

How are you doing?

How many points have you got? Put two crosses on the chart: one for grammar and one for vocabulary.

	1	2	3	4	5	6	7	8	9	10	11	12	13
Grammar													

	1	2	3	4	5	6	7	8	9	10	11	12	13
Vocabulary													

2 Vocabulary

a Put the letters in the correct order and make words for natural disasters.

1 nasutmi ....
2 rhtugdo ....
3 anevchala ....
4 covlanic reupiont ....
5 anehicrur ....
6 odlof ....
7 quathaeker .... [7]

b Complete the sentences with the words in the box.

anorak   fleece   goggles   insect repellent
rucksack   sun cream   torch   wetsuit

1 It's dark outside – take a ....
2 The water's cold – you should wear a
  ....
3 .... will keep the mosquitoes away.
4 I always put on .... when it's sunny.
5 Take an .... – it might rain.
6 I'll carry everything in my ....
7 A .... is warm but quite light to carry.
8 I always wear .... to protect my
  eyes when I'm skiing. [8]

c Circle the correct words.

1 Don't *be cross / make up* with me – it was
  an accident!
2 I'll *let / get* my parents down if I fail my exams.
3 You should always stick up *with / for* your friends.
4 If you do that again, I'll *tell on / get on* you!
5 I *had / made* an argument with my parents.
6 I like Sam. I *get on / let on* really well with him.
7 It's horrible when you *fall out / get on* with your
  friends!
8 She's my best friend, so I'll try and make *up for /
  up with* her.
9 Do you *get on / stick up* well with Tom? [9]

GREEN:	Great! Tell your teacher your score!
YELLOW:	Not bad, but go to the website for extra practice.
RED:	Talk to your teacher and look at Units 3 and 4 again. Go to the website for extra practice.

14	15	16	17	18	19	20	21	22	23	24	25	26	27	28	29	30

14	15	16	17	18	19	20	21	22	23	24	25	26	27	28	29	30

d Complete the crossword.

Across

3 Able to understand people's feelings.
5 Relaxed.
6 Willing to help other people.

Down

1 Someone who is .... doesn't show respect.
2 Don't shout at your parents – it's .... !
4 It's .... to say please and thank you.

[6]

Correct it!

Correct these typical learner errors
from Units 3 and 4.

1 We're go to the beach next Saturday.
  ....

2 What will you do at four o'clock this afternoon?
  Would it be a good time to talk?
  ....

3 They'll have a picnic next weekend.
  ....

4 We're going pass all our exams this year.
  ....

5 At six o'clock tomorrow we be taking the exam.
  ....

6 The day at the theme park was funny!
  ....

7 I will buy the dress unless I get a pay rise.
  ....

8 What will you do if you won $5000 in a quiz show?
  ....

9 If you do more exercise, you'd feel better.
  ....

10 As soon that the water boils, add the pasta.
  ....

Permission: *can*, *let* and *be allowed to*
Passive review
Vocabulary: School; Memory
Interaction 5: Interrupting

1 Read and listen

a Read the text quickly and match the headings with the paragraphs A–C.

Lessons or no lessons?   Do it yourself   Transcendental meditation

Lessons in life

Many schools in the UK are experimenting with new ways of learning. We visited a few of them.

A ....

Who needs teachers when you have the internet? In an experiment at Eggbuckland School, in Devon, a group of secondary students were allowed to take control of their own learning. They researched lessons using laptops and then taught each other. The teachers let them make mistakes and didn't correct them at all.

The students soon learned to look at several internet sites while preparing their lessons. Dan Buckley, the head teacher, said the students gave excellent lessons.

How did the laptop group get on compared with students in other classes? At the end of the first year, the independent learners got worse marks than students in traditional classes. But after two years they all got higher grades in their final exams.

B ....

Freddy Fuller meditates for 45 minutes, morning and evening, with two other 15-minute sessions during the day. He says it calms him down and helps him focus on schoolwork. Freddy, aged 16, attends a small private school in Lancashire. All students at the school meditate silently for 10 minutes at the beginning and end of the day. They can meditate for longer if they want. The school's exam results are twice as good as the national average.

The St James' Independent School, in London, also has daily meditation for all its students. The head teacher, David Boddy, thinks that meditation helps students concentrate in class, but believes that listening to music or playing video games has the opposite effect. The students aren't allowed to use MP3 players in school. At St James', every class starts and finishes with a 30-second silence, so students can prepare their minds for studying.

C ....

Summerhill, in Suffolk, is famous for being different. It is called 'the school where you don't have to go to lessons' or 'the school with no rules'. But there are a lot of rules. The difference is that rules are made at the school council, where all the teachers and pupils have one vote each. However, the council doesn't let students do everything they want. For example, the punishment for writing graffiti on the walls is a £2 fine.

And do students have to go to lessons? Chae-Eun Park, a 16-year-old student from South Korea, explains that students can choose which lessons they want to attend. She thinks that students learn to be confident and responsible because they are allowed to make choices for themselves. As a result, Summerhill's exam results are impressive.

b 🔊 2.2 Read the text again and listen. Write A, B or C.

1 Silence is part of the school day. ....
2 Teachers didn't correct students' mistakes. ....
3 Students don't have to attend lessons. ....
4 Students and teachers decide about the rules together. ....
5 Students taught each other. ....
6 Students can't listen to their MP3 players. ....

c Work with a partner. Answer the questions.

1 Which of these schools would you like to go to?

2 What changes would you like to make to your school? Why?

2 Vocabulary

School

a 🔊 **2.3** Match the words with the definitions. Then listen and check.

> **1** be in detention **2** cheat **3** come top in
> **4** fail **5** a high mark **6** pass **7** retake
> **8** revise **9** skive off (informal) **10** term

A to be successful in an exam

B a good result for an essay or a project

C the school year is divided into three of these

D to study something before a test or exam

E to behave in a dishonest way in an exam

F to get a bad result in an exam or a test

G to be the best in the class or school at a subject

H to not go to school when you should

I to be kept in school after class as a punishment

J to do an exam again

b 🔊 **2.4** Listen to these students and teachers and (circle) the correct words.

1 Sandra and Anna got *low / high* marks.

2 Anna *revised for / cheated in* the test.

3 Joe has to *revise / be in detention* at the weekend.

4 Joe will have to *study for / retake* an exam.

5 Chris *passed / failed* his exam.

6 Chris got 65% in his *French / Maths* exam.

7 Lucy is *cheating in / retaking* an exam.

8 Lucy will have to see the *head teacher / English teacher*.

c Work with a partner. Answer the questions.

1 How do you prepare for exams? Do you spend a lot of time revising?

2 Is it important for you to pass exams and get high marks? Why? / Why not?

Culture Vulture

Did you know that in England and Wales students usually study about ten subjects until they are 16? They then study three or four subjects between the ages of 16 and 18. How many subjects do students study at 16–18 in your country? Do you think they study too many or too few subjects?

3 Speak

a Work in pairs.
Student A: Read the instructions and write words or numbers in the shapes.
Student B: Turn to page 124.

1 In the triangle write your favourite subject.

2 In the square write your best mark in the last two weeks.

3 In the circle write the length of the morning break at your school.

4 In the rectangle write the number of languages you are learning.

5 In the oval write your least favourite school day of the week.

b Look at your partner's shapes and guess what the words or numbers mean. Ask follow-up questions if possible.

> ⤏ A: *Maths. Is that your favourite subject?*
> B: *No, it isn't. Try again.*

(4) Grammar

Permission: *can, let* and *be allowed to*

a Look at the examples. Then (circle) the correct words to complete the rules.

> ⌁ *Students* **were allowed to take** *control of their own learning.*
> *The teachers* **let** *them* **make** *mistakes.*
> *They* **can meditate** *for longer if they want.*
>
> ● We use *can* and *be allowed to* when someone tells us it is **OK / not OK** to do something.
> ● We use *let* when we tell someone it is **OK / not OK** to do something.
> ● We use *let* + person + **verb / verb + -*ing*.

Grammar reference: Workbook page 90

b Read the texts and choose the correct answer: A, B or C.

Should a 17-year-old girl ¹ .... wear a tuxedo to her high-school prom (formal end-of-year party)? Her school principal in Indiana, USA, says that girls ² .... wear tuxedos and she must wear a dress instead.

UPDATE: The school has changed its decision and this year it will ³ .... female students wear tuxedos.

To show how much he loves his team, the Cincinnati Bengals, Dustin Reader shaved the letter 'B' into his hair. His school, however, ⁴ .... students come to class with unusual hairstyles. School officials say he will ⁵ .... come back to school when his hair grows back, or when he changes his hairstyle.

1	**A** can	**B** be allowed to	**C** let
2	**A** can	**B** not allowed to	**C** can't
3	**A** can	**B** be allowed to	**C** let
4	**A** is allowed to	**B** doesn't let	**C** can't
5	**A** be allowed to	**B** can	**C** let

Check it out!

● *Let* is followed by the verb without *to*.
They don't **let us wear** earrings.
NOT ~~They don't let us to wear earrings.~~

c Change the words in *italics* if necessary, so that they are true for your school.

1 We *can* wear jeans to school.
2 We *aren't allowed to* go outside in the breaks.
3 We *are allowed to* chew gum in class.
4 The teachers *let* us smoke in school.
5 We *can't* bring our own food to school.
6 The teacher *lets* us talk in our own language in English classes.

d Work in a group. Answer the questions.

1 Should teenagers be allowed to wear what they want at school or at school events?
2 Do you think parents should let teenagers stay out late at the weekend?
3 Should parents let teenagers have parties without adult supervision?

(5) Pronunciation 〔DVD〕

Final *e*

a 〔🔊〕2.5 An *e* at the end of a word can change the pronunciation. Listen and repeat the words.

b 〔🔊〕2.5 Listen again and match the words to the sounds.

1	mad	/eɪ/		**7**	not	/əʊ/
2	made	/æ/		**8**	note	/ɒ/
3	pet	/e/		**9**	us	/ʌ/
4	Pete	/iː/		**10**	use	/uː/
5	sit	/aɪ/				
6	site	/ɪ/				

c Look at the words. Can you guess the pronunciation with a final *e*?

1	at		**4**	fin
2	bit		**5**	pin
3	tap		**6**	hat

d 〔🔊〕2.6 Listen, check and repeat.

e 〔🔊〕2.7 Listen and repeat.

When I revise, I use a computer and complete my notes before I take the exam.

6 Vocabulary

Memory

a 🔊 **2.8** Match the words or phrases in **bold** with the definitions. Which two have the same meaning? Then listen and check.

1 Ben's got a good **memory**. He can always remember lots of information, even in exams.

2 Susie's very good at Maths as well as languages. She's got a great **mind**.

3 I've written myself a message so I won't **forget** to do my essay.

4 I'm playing the leading role in the school play, so I've got to **memorise** a lot of lines.

5 **Remind** me to take my sports kit to school.

6 The teacher told us to **learn** this poem **by heart**.

A the opposite of 'remember'

B the ability to remember things

C learn something so that you will remember it exactly (2 answers)

D the part of a person that enables a person to think, feel emotions and be aware of things

E tell someone else to remember something

Check it out!

- If you *remember* something, you don't forget it. If you *remind* someone else about something, you tell them so that they don't forget.
  I must **remember** to post the letter.
  Remind me to post the letter. (= tell me)
  NOT ~~Remember me to post the letter.~~

b Complete the sentences. Use the words in Exercise 6a.

1 Einstein had a brilliant _____ .

2 I must _____ to do my Maths homework for Wednesday.

3 Don't _____ to phone me later.

4 Did you _____ the words to the song? We have to sing it at the concert tomorrow evening.

5 My grandmother's _____ is getting worse. She often forgets my name.

6 _____ me to post that letter.

c Work with a partner. Answer the questions.

1 Have you got a good memory?

2 How do you memorise things?

3 How do you remember new English words?

4 What things do you forget?

7 Listen

a Work with a partner. Do the quiz.

1 **How much sleep do teenagers need?**
   A 7 hours   B 8 hours   C 9 hours

2 **Teenagers are most awake in the …**
   A evening   B morning   C afternoon

3 **Deep REM (Rapid Eye Movement) sleep is necessary because it helps with …**
   A memory   B stress   C A and B

4 **Your brain changes more when you're in your …**
   A teens   B twenties   C thirties

5 **People learn best …**
   A by memorising   B in different   C by writing
      information   ways   notes

b 🔊 **2.9** Listen to part of a talk by Dr Laura Baker, an expert on the brain. Check your answers to Exercise 7a.

c 🔊 **2.9** Listen again. Are the sentences *right* (✓) or *wrong* (✗)? Correct the wrong sentences.

1 People need the same amount of sleep throughout their lives.

2 REM sleep is very important at exam times.

3 A teenager's brain changes less than an adult's brain.

4 Practising a variety of activities isn't good for your brain.

5 It's more difficult to learn things as an adult.

6 Everyone learns in the same way.

d Work with a partner. Discuss the questions.

1 What time of day do you learn best?

2 What different things do you do to use your brain?

(8) Grammar

Passive review

a Look at the examples. Then (circle) the correct words to complete the rules.

> ⤷ Sleep **is needed** for lots of reasons.
> Lots of connections **are built** between brain cells.
> I **wasn't taught** to play a musical instrument.
> A lot of studies **have been done** about the importance of sleep.
> This book **was written** by an expert on sleep.

- We use a passive verb when we **know** / **don't know** who did something, or the action is **more** / **less** important than who does it.
- We form the passive with the verb *be* and the **past participle** / **-ing form**.
- The verb *be* **can** / **cannot** be in any tense.
- We can say who did something with **by** / **for**.

Grammar reference: Workbook page 90

Check it out!

- We can use modals + *be* + past participle (e.g. *will, might, can, should*).
  Food **should not be eaten** in the library.
  The repairs **might be finished** soon.

b Rewrite the sentences in the passive.

1 People don't use mobile phones in our class.

....

2 Scientists have done research to show how the brain works.

....

3 They sold all the concert tickets before 11:00.

....

4 We can do this later.

....

5 They will release the new version of the game next month.

....

6 When did they invent the telephone?

....

7 They don't sell pizzas in that restaurant.

....

Interaction 5 DVD

Interrupting

a 🔊 **2.10** Listen to Mike, George and Ella talking about school. Tick (✓) the thing they agree is the most important at school.

b 🔊 **2.10** Complete the phrases with the words. Then listen again and check.

> course   finish   go on   hang   point
> something

Interrupting
Sorry, can I just say .... ?
Can I make a .... here?

Allowing someone to interrupt
Yeah, ...
Yes, of ....

Not allowing someone to interrupt
.... on a minute.
Can I just .... ?

c Work in a group of four.
Student A: Turn to page 119.
Student B: Turn to page 122.

Portfolio 5

Ideas for improving your school

a Read the memo from the headteacher and the two letters with suggestions. Which letter do you think is better? Why?

Memo

From: The headteacher

To: All students in the school

We have recently received some money from the government and we would like your ideas on how to improve the school. Please write to Ms Brown, the Deputy Headteacher, with your suggestions and reasons for making the improvements. She will write back to you with the final decision.

b Read the second letter again and look at the phrases in **bold**. How does the writer …

1 start the letter?
2 explain the reason for writing?
3 put the parts of the letter in order?
4 finish the letter?
5 say goodbye at the end?

Check it out!

- In formal letters:
  If you don't know the name, use **Dear Sir/Madam**, and **Yours faithfully** at the end.
  If you know the name, use **Dear Mr/Ms White**, and **Yours sincerely** at the end.

c Look at the phrases in *italics* in the second letter. Find three ways to …

1 give opinions.
2 make suggestions.

d Write a letter explaining how your school could be improved and why it should be improved. Include:

- three ideas for changes and reasons why they are necessary
- language from Exercise c
- the features of formal letters from Exercise b

e Read your partner's letter. Do you agree with your partner's ideas?

---

① Hi there

Let me give you a few ideas. First off, we need a much bigger science lab and you should let the younger kids use it. The equipment's really old, too. And another thing – we need more computers so everybody can do their homework in the library. Not everyone has a computer at home, you know! Before I finish, I want to say that it would be cool if we could talk more to teachers. A school council for students and teachers would be great.

OK, that's all. Write back soon.

Cheers,

Ally J

② **Dear Ms Brown**

I am writing to explain how I think the school can be improved.

Firstly, *I think* we should improve the science facilities. *In my opinion* we need two new science laboratories with more modern equipment. At the moment there is only one laboratory and younger students are not allowed to use it because it is used by the older students every day.

Another point is that there are not enough computers in the libraries. Many students would like to do their homework there and not everyone has a computer at home. *I recommend* buying a lot more computers.

Finally, *I'd like to say* that I think *we should* have more discussion between teachers and students. *We could* have a school council meeting every month to talk about important issues. The school council would be able to plan ways of raising money for things like new computers.

I hope these ideas are useful. **I look forward to hearing from you soon.**

Yours sincerely,

Jack Walker (Class 5B)

6 Who's got talent?

Past perfect
Past perfect continuous
Vocabulary: Noun suffixes;
Entertainment collocations
Interaction 6: Agreeing and disagreeing

1 Read and listen

a Look at the photos. What types of TV programmes are they from?

Young and talented

TV talent shows are one of the most popular types of entertainment on television these days, but it's not just singers and dancers who share their talent with studio audiences and viewers at home.

1 ....

At the age of 22, Abdi Farah won the reality TV show *Work of Art* with his artistic creations. The prize was his very own exhibition at the world-famous Brooklyn Museum in New York and over $100,000. During the competition, Abdi created many paintings and photographs, but his sculptures of athletes and self-portraits were what won him the title of 'The Next Great Artist'. For Abdi, taking part in the show was the greatest artistic experience of his life. Before the show, he had expected to learn about business and working with people, but he found that he actually learned a lot about art itself. In his opinion, one of the best things about the show is that viewers are able to follow the development of the works of art from the beginning, when they are just ideas, to the finished product.

2 ....

18-year-old Emily Ludolf was still at school when she appeared on the TV cookery show *Masterchef*. Even though she didn't win, the young finalist impressed the judges with her imagination and creativity in the kitchen. It's a tough competition; contestants are filmed for a month, sometimes 22 hours a day. They are given a selection of food and only have a few minutes to decide what to cook and how to cook it. For the contestants, part of the excitement is not knowing what the final dish will taste like, but Emily amazed everyone with her talent for combining unusual flavours. Emily had visited South Africa, Morocco and Cuba before she was on *Masterchef* and she used ideas from these places in her recipes. Emily's ambitions are to travel and learn more about food from other cultures, become a food writer and one day have her own restaurant.

3 ....

American fashion designer Christian Siriano has designed clothes for everyone from Heidi Klum to Lady Gaga. He became famous after his appearance on the TV reality show *Project Runway*, where contestants have to design clothes in a limited amount of time. During the show, the 21-year-old won more challenges than any other participant. Through his hard work and determination Christian won first prize and presented his collection at New York Fashion Week, where he now presents regularly. Before going on *Project Runway*, Christian was familiar with the fashion industry as he had worked as a make-up artist, a wedding dress designer and for British designers Vivienne Westwood and Alexander McQueen. Since winning the show, he has started his own successful business and his designs have appeared in the most important fashion magazines around the world.

b Read the text quickly and match paragraphs 1–3 with photos A–C.

c 🔊 **2.12** Read the text again and listen. Then answer the questions.
1 What did Abdi learn on the show?
2 What does Abdi like most about the show?
3 Why did the judges like Emily's cooking?
4 What does Emily want to do in the future?
5 What jobs did Christian do before the show?
6 How has Christian's life changed since he won the show?

d Find the words in the text that mean ...
1 known by many people around the world (para 1)
2 pictures you paint of yourself (para 1)
3 difficult (para 2)
4 different from others or strange (para 2)
5 difficult tasks (para 3)
6 a dress that a woman wears when she gets married (para 3)

e Work in a group. Answer the questions.
1 Which of the three TV reality shows would you most like to take part in? Why?
2 Do you think reality TV shows are a good way of discovering talented people? Why? / Why not?

2 Vocabulary

Noun suffixes

a 🔊 **2.13** We can add suffixes to words to make nouns. Look at the examples and write them in the tables. Then listen and check.

> appearance   artist   creation   entertainment
> reality   ~~singer~~

People	
verb + -er	noun + -ist
singer	

Things, feelings, qualities			
verb + -(t)ion	verb + -ment	verb + -ance	adj + -ity

b 🔊 **2.14** Add noun suffixes to the words in the box and add them to the tables in Exercise 2a. Then listen and check.

> creative   design   excite   exhibit   final
> perform   select   style

c Complete the sentences with the correct form of the words in Exercise 2b.

1 I love .... like Galliano and Versace. Their clothes are amazing.
2 There were three .... in the competition, but only one winner.
3 Have you seen the new photography .... at the city art museum?
4 There's a wonderful .... of dishes on the menu. It's difficult to choose.
5 I love watching her on stage – she's a great ....!
6 She works as a hair .... for models at fashion shows.
7 There was a lot of .... in the studio while they chose the winning design.
8 It takes a lot of .... to come up with such good ideas.

d Work in a group. Answer the questions.

1 Which artists or fashion designers do you like? Why?
2 What kinds of exhibition do you like going to see?
3 What types of entertainment do you like watching on TV?

Culture Vulture

Did you know that 'Britain's Got Talent' is a popular TV talent show in Britain? In 2009 over 19 million viewers, around 32% of the whole population, watched the show. Which TV talent shows are popular in your country? Which reality TV shows do you watch?

3 Pronunciation

Changing word stress

a 🔊 **2.15** When we add a noun suffix to a word, the stress can move to a different syllable. Listen to the word stress in these examples.

compe<u>te</u> – compe<u>ti</u>tion
i<u>ma</u>gine – imagi<u>na</u>tion
<u>pho</u>tograph – pho<u>to</u>grapher

b 🔊 **2.16** Listen to the pairs of words and <u>underline</u> the stressed syllables in the nouns column. Then tick (✓) the words if the word stress moves.

		Nouns	Word stress moves? ✓
1	<u>dance</u>	dancer	
2	cre<u>a</u>tive	creativity	
3	enter<u>tain</u>	entertainment	
4	<u>fin</u>al	finalist	
5	ex<u>hib</u>it	exhibition	
6	<u>real</u>	reality	
7	de<u>vel</u>op	development	
8	<u>edu</u>cate	education	
9	<u>ac</u>tive	activity	
10	de<u>sign</u>	designer	

Check it out!

- Nouns ending in -ion or -ity usually stress the syllable before the suffix.
  col**lec**tion, simi**lar**ity
- Nouns ending in -ment and -ness usually keep the same stress.
  enjoy – en**joy**ment
  happy – **ha**ppiness

c 🔊 **2.17** Listen and repeat.

The artists, photographers and designers created amazing collections for their exhibitions.

(4) Grammar

Past perfect

a Look at the examples. Write 1 or 2 next to sentences to put the events in order.

> ⟶ *Emily had visited South Africa, Morocco and Cuba before she was on* Masterchef.
> *Before going on* Project Runway, *Christian had worked as a make-up artist.*
>
> Emily went to South Africa, Morocco and Cuba. ☐
>
> Emily was on *Masterchef*. ☐
>
> Christian was on *Project Runway*. ☐
>
> Christian worked as a make-up artist. ☐
>
> (Circle) the correct words to complete the rules.
> - We use the past perfect to emphasise that an action happened **before / at the same time as** another action in the past.
> - We form the past perfect with **have / had** and the past participle.

Grammar reference: Workbook page 80

b Complete the sentences with the past simple or past perfect form of the verbs and the time expressions.

In 2010, 19-year-old Charlie Bruce [1].................(win) the British TV talent show *So you think you can dance*. Over 6 million viewers [2].................(watch) the show. Before her audition Charlie [3]................. (already/decide) that this would be her last audition because she [4].................(attend) lots of auditions before, but she [5].................(never/be) successful. Before she [6].................(appear) on the show Charlie [7].................(not be) able to get a job as a dancer, so she [8].................(work) in a shop.

(5) Vocabulary

Entertainment collocations

a 🔊)) **2.18** Match a word from each box to make entertainment collocations. Then listen and check.

| 1 art 2 fashion 3 media 4 natural 5 prize |
| 6 reality 7 sports 8 studio 9 talent |
| 10 world |

| **A** attention **B** audience **C** champion |
| **D** designer **E** money **F** museum **G** show |
| **H** star **I** talent **J** TV |

b Complete the sentences with the correct form of the collocations in Exercise 5a.

1 I think .... like footballers and basketball players are overpaid.
2 Have you seen that .... show about people who learn a new sport?
3 Have you ever watched a live TV show sitting in the .... ?
4 My favourite .... are in Paris. I love the Louvre and the Musée d'Orsay.
5 I would never wear any clothes by that .... – they're too unusual.
6 He's the .... because he's won more tournaments than any other player.
7 She's definitely got a .... for singing. Her voice is amazing.
8 How many participants are in tonight's .... ?

c Complete the sentences so they are true for you.

1 I think reality TV is ...
2 If I could meet a sports star, I'd love to meet ...
3 I've got a natural talent for ...

d Work with a partner. Answer the questions.

1 How much prize money do you think the winner of a TV talent show should win?
2 Why do you think some fashion designers design crazy clothes?
3 Why do some reality TV contestants get so much media attention?

(6) Listen

a What activities can you see in the photos? Which do you think you need natural talent to do?

b 🔊 2.19 Listen to four people talking about talent. What does each speaker think is more important: natural talent or practice? Listen and write *T* (talent) or *P* (practice).

1 Katia ....   2 Carlos ....   3 Hannah ....   4 Jack ....

c 🔊 2.19 Listen again. Choose the correct answer: A, B or C.

1 What does Katia have a natural talent for?
    A reading   **B** hip hop dancing
    C reading and hip hop dancing

2 Carlos thinks that people will practise a lot if they …
    A have a lot of free time   **B** want to be the best
    C like something

3 Hannah's friend …
    A sings and plays the piano
    B sings in a band   **C** wants to be on TV

4 What does Jack think the best world champions need to do?
    A start when they are young
    B have natural talent   **C** practise a lot

d Work with a partner. Answer the questions.

1 What do you think is more important: natural talent or practice? Why?

2 Who do you know who is very good at something? Do they have natural talent or do they practise a lot?

(7) Speak

a Work with a partner. Ask your partner questions and complete the table. Use the prompts to help you.

- what/you/do/free time? *What do you do in your free time?*
- when/you/start ....-*ing*?
- how often/you .... ?

- difficult or easy to learn?
- you/have to/practise a lot?
- you/good at ....-*ing*?

Name	Free-time activities: music, dance, acting, sport, computers, other	Hours/day	Hours/week
Lara	*Hip hop dancing.* *She started when she was 11.* *It was difficult to learn.* *She has to practise a lot.* *She's good at dancing.*		*10*

b Tell your class about your partner's free-time activity. Use your notes to help you.

(8) Grammar

Past perfect continuous

a Look at the examples and answer the questions.

> ···➤ *I'd been reading for a year* before I started school.
> She**'d been singing** in a girl band for ages before she started lessons.
> His dad **had been teaching** him the keyboard and violin since he was three.

1 Could I read when I started school?
2 What did I do first, learn to read or start school?

Circle the correct words to complete the rules.

● We use the past perfect continuous for a longer past action that was happening **before** / **after** another action in the past.
● We often use the past perfect continuous with *for* / *since* + period of time and *for* / *since* + a point in time.
● We form the past perfect continuous with *had* + *been* + *-ing* / *-ed* form.

Grammar reference: Workbook page 80

b Complete the sentences with the verbs in the past perfect continuous and *for* or *since*.

1 Mozart .... (learn) music .... five years when he wrote his first symphony.
2 Michael Jordan .... (play) with the Chicago Bulls .... nine years when he retired in 1993.
3 When Jodie Foster won an Oscar in 1991, she .... (act) .... 26 years.
4 By 1506, Leonardo da Vinci .... (paint) the *Mona Lisa* .... almost three years.
5 When Mary Quant, the fashion designer, invented the mini skirt in 1965 she .... (sell) clothes in her own shop .... 1965.

Check it out!

● We use the past perfect continuous to show that an action continued over a period of time.
● We use the past perfect simple when we say how many times it happened.

I'd been studying Spanish for over a year.
I'd been to Spain three times before.
NOT ~~I'd been going to Spain three times before.~~

c Circle the correct words.

1 She had *looked / been looking* for her keys for over an hour before she found them.
2 I had already *met / been meeting* my best friend before I started school.
3 I couldn't go to the cinema because I had *lost / been losing* my wallet.
4 I got to the concert late, but luckily the band hadn't *played / been playing* for long.
5 When I saw Jane I could see that she *had cried / had been crying*.
6 I didn't go to the cinema with the others because I *had seen / had been seeing* that film before.

Interaction 6

Agreeing and disagreeing

a 🔊 **2.20** Listen to Mia and Peter talking about TV talent shows. Write *M* (Mia) or *P* (Peter) next to their opinions.

TV talent shows …
1 are an opportunity to become famous. ☐
2 give false hope and disappointment. ☐
3 attract positive media attention. ☐

b 🔊 **2.20** Listen again. Tick (✓) the phrases you hear.

1 I see what you mean, but … ☐
2 I totally disagree! ☐
3 That's completely untrue! ☐
4 OK, maybe you've got a point. ☐
5 I agree with what you're saying, but … ☐
6 Yes, I hadn't thought of that. ☐
7 Yes, absolutely! ☐
8 Yes, definitely, but … ☐

c Work with a partner.

Student A: Turn to page 119.
Student B: Turn to page 122.

Portfolio 6

Completing a form

a Read the magazine page. What's the competition for? What can you win?

b Now read Mickey's nomination form. Who does he nominate? Why?

Talk talk magazine competition!

Talent award

Do you know anyone at school or in your family with an amazing talent? Nominate them to win. We have three prizes of £500!

We are looking for young people (aged 14–20) who ...

- have a natural talent for something
- have worked hard to develop their talent
- have clear plans for the future

Click here to complete your **nomination form**

Next month's competition Volunteers with a difference.

What would you like to nominate the person for?

Arts and music ☐   Sport and fitness ✓   Other ☐

Nominator: Name: Mickey   **Surname:** Jones   **Age:** 16

How do you know the nominee?   Best friend
1 ....   Since we were 12.

Nominee: Name: Shaun 2 .... Baxter **Age:** 16

What is the nominee's talent?   Swimming and water polo

3 ....

Brenthill sports club, Brenthill swimming and water polo club, King William school swimming and water polo team, Wales under-18s swimming and water polo teams. Great Britain under-18s swimming and water polo teams.

4 ....

When I first met Shaun, he'd been swimming since he was six and he'd already won several competitions. Since then, he's also won silver and gold medals for Wales in swimming and water polo. He took part in the 2010 youth Olympics in Singapore.

5 ....

Shaun gets up every morning at 4:30 and swims for two hours before school. Then he plays water polo two evenings a week and works out at the gym twice a week. I think he's got a natural talent for swimming, but he also trains a lot.

6 ....

Shaun wants to swim for Britain in the next Olympics and he's already in training! He also wants to get into sports college next year.

Why do you believe the nominee should get this award?
Shaun had already been working hard at his sport before I met him four years ago. I think it's amazing that he can be a normal student at school, have time to do his school work, train outside school and never get stressed out.

c Some questions and headings are missing from the form. Write words and sentences A–F in gaps 1–6 on the form.

- **A** How has the nominee worked hard at their talent?
- **B** Surname:
- **C** What are the nominee's plans for the future?
- **D** What important things has the nominee done?
- **E** Which groups or clubs is the nominee a member of?
- **F** How long have you known the nominee?

d Write a nomination form to nominate someone you know for the award. Include the same headings and questions as Mickey's form.

e Read other nominations in your class and choose three winners. Why do you think they should win?

1

food & drink

LIFE'S GOOD
FOOD'S GREAT

FOOD options at the NIA

The NIA offers a wide choice of good-quality food.

- a selection of food, drink and confectionery outlets
- hot food, including jacket potatoes, burgers and pizzas
- snacks and sandwiches
- all food and drink areas open at the advertised 'doors open' time for the show
- enjoy food and drink in the food areas, or take it to your seat

2

the nia
birmingham

The Birmingham National Indoor Arena (NIA) is one of the busiest indoor sporting and entertainment venues in Europe. Since it opened in 1991, it has welcomed visitors to over 30 different sports, and a huge variety of entertainment and music.

The NIA has played host to artists such as Prince, Coldplay and Destiny's Child. It has also hosted many other forms of entertainment, including the spectacular *Disney on Ice* shows, *Lord of the Dance* and the *Cirque du Soleil*.

3

GORILLAZ

At the NIA Friday 10 September
Tickets £35–45 (All prices exclude fees and charges)

Doors: 17:00 **Show:** 19:30
See the NIA website for more details

4

DIVERSITY

See this amazing 10-piece street dance troupe perform at the NIA on

Saturday 11 December!

Spectacular dance routines that incorporate many different styles of music, from classical to hip-hop.

'Energetic and eye-catching – pure entertainment'

The best entertainment this Christmas!

Tickets are priced at £21.50 and are available from the Ticket Factory, on **0844 338 8000** or online at www.theticketfactory.com

5

GB JUDO WORLD CUP
for Men and Women

This year, for the first time, Great Britain will hold a Judo World Cup for both men and women. It will be the biggest Judo World Cup ever held in Britain.

At: The National Indoor Arena, Birmingham

Tickets
£14 (adults)
£6 (children and senior citizens)

6

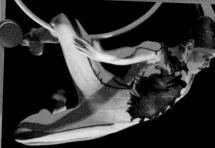

Cirque du Soleil
QUIDAM

Coming soon to the National Indoor Arena, Birmingham

A dramatic mix of circus arts and street entertainment.

Cirque du Soleil is no ordinary circus – don't miss this unique show, seen in over 20 countries.

Book early to avoid disappointment!

1 Culture UK: Birmingham's National Indoor Arena

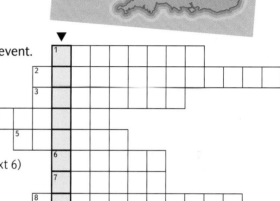

a Look at the information about the National Indoor Arena (NIA) in Birmingham and answer the questions.

1 Who are Diversity and how many members are there?
2 Where can you get tickets to see Diversity?
3 What is special about the judo world cup this year?
4 Who performed at the NIA in September?
5 How many countries has Cirque du Soleil performed in?
6 What types of food can you buy at the NIA?
7 Where can you eat food at the NIA?
8 How long has the NIA been open?

Birmingham

b Complete the crossword and find an international type of event.

1 received (visitors) (text 2)
2 sweet food or chocolates (text 1)
3 normal or usual (text 6)
4 a shop that sells the products of one company (text 1)
5 .... events take place inside a building (text 2)
6 a show where acrobats perform in a tent called a Big Top (text 6)
7 the only one of its kind (text 6)
8 very exciting to look at or watch (text 4)

c Work with a partner. Look at the information about the NIA. Which events would you most like to see? Why?

2 Your project

An events calendar

a Work in a group. Make a list of different types of event.

b Use the internet or local newspapers and magazines to make a list of future events where you live. Find out about:

- the type of event (concert, sports event, theatre show, etc.)
- the venue
- the date(s), time and ticket prices
- specific information about the event (performers, what happens, why it's being held, etc.)

c Make an events calendar for where you live. Circle the dates on a calendar and write information about five or six events. Include the information from Exercise 2b.

South Korea Festivals!

Gangneung Danoje Festival
This is one of Korea's oldest festivals. Celebrating Korean traditional culture, there will be dancing, parades, wrestling and bidding farewell to the gods on the last of the 8 days.

Muju Firefly Festival
A great free festival if you enjoy hands-on activities, such as trout fishing and rafting. Muju's fireflies are famous in South Korea – this is your chance to see them up close.

World Taekwondo Culture Expo
Held in the Muju-gun area. A five-day event which attracts Taekwondo fans from all over the world. For $150 you can participate, watch displays and learn from the best.

Busan International Rock Festival
Over 150,000 people attend this free music festival every year. For two days you can rock to established and debut artists from sunrise to sunset.

January February
March April
May June
July August
September October
November December

Boryeong Mud Festival
A fantastic fun festival which is firmly established on the international calendar. Enjoy mud-wrestling, mud-massages, mud-sliding, mud-swimming, mud-assault-courses and many more mud activities!

Busan International Film Festival
One of Asia's foremost film festivals is held right here in South Korea. Very popular with the youth who attend in large numbers.

Review ⑤ and ⑥

① Grammar

a Look at the school rules then circle the correct words.

✔ You have permission to …	✗ You do not have permission to …
sit in a classroom in break time bring your own food for lunch	run inside the school eat or drink during classes use mobile phones during classes write on the walls or desks

1 If you don't want to go outside in the break, you *can / can't* sit in a classroom.

2 You *are / aren't* allowed to run inside the school.

3 You *can / can't* use your mobile phone in class.

4 You *are / aren't* allowed to bring your own lunch.

5 The teachers *let / don't let* you eat during classes.

6 You *can / can't* write on the walls! ☐ 6

b Complete the second sentence so that it means the same as the first. Use the word in brackets.

1 We can't talk during exams.
   We .... (allowed) during exams.

2 I'm not allowed to use my dad's computer.
   My dad doesn't .... (let) his computer.

3 I can't watch TV after ten o'clock.
   I .... (allowed) TV after ten o'clock. ☐ 6

c Complete the sentences with the verbs in the correct form of the passive.

1 Penicillin .... (discover) in 1928.

2 Drama classes .... (offer) at our school every year.

3 A lot of books .... (write) on this subject already.

4 .... the computer room .... (use) every day?

5 A lot of improvements .... (make) to the school since I came here.

6 The video .... (make) last year. ☐ 6

d Complete the sentences with the past simple, past perfect or past perfect continuous form of the verbs.

1 She .... (play) the guitar for ages before she started having lessons.

2 I .... (meet) my best friend about seven years ago.

3 How long .... you .... (know) him before you got married?

4 Mick .... (cycle) for two hours when he had an accident.

5 When we arrived at the airport the plane .... already .... (leave).

6 They .... (write) for 50 minutes when the teacher told them to stop. ☐ 6

e Read the text and choose the correct answer: A, B or C.

Tinchy Stryder is a very unusual pop star. He is the first person who [1]....... a number one single in the UK charts with the title 'Number 1', and he is probably the first pop star to have to write a 6,000-word essay during a tour. Tinchy had his number one hit in 2009, at the age of 21, but he [2]....... rap since the age of 14 and he [3]....... out his debut album (Star in the Hood) two years [4]....... . Although he [5]....... to be a musician, he started a course in animation at the University of East London. While on tour last year he [6]....... a documentary film as part of his course work.

1 A had   B has had   C has
2 A performed   B was performing   C had been performing
3 A had brought   B has brought   C having brought
4 A soon   B earlier   C later
5 A always wants   B always had wanted C had always wanted
6 A has made   B had made   C made ☐ 6

How are you doing?

How many points have you got? Put two crosses on the chart: one for grammar and one for vocabulary.

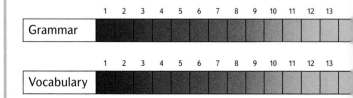

	1	2	3	4	5	6	7	8	9	10	11	12	13
Grammar													

	1	2	3	4	5	6	7	8	9	10	11	12	13
Vocabulary													

② Vocabulary

a Match the two parts of the sentences.

1 Daisy failed her exam ☐

2 Emily passed all her exams ☐

3 I can't go out tonight because ☐

4 Sam got a high mark in the test ☐

5 I was caught cheating, ☐

6 I am in trouble because ☐

A so she's going to university.

B I have to revise for the test tomorrow.

C so he's going out to celebrate.

D and that's why I'm in detention.

E I skived off PE.

F so she will have to retake it. ☐ 6

b Complete the crossword about memory.
Use the clues to help you.

Across

4 People often .... the words to songs
.... (3 words)

6 Don't .... to ring me later!

Down

1 If your .... is good, you can remember
lots of things.

2 Yoga is good for your body and your ....

3 I had to .... a whole poem for the exam.

5 Can you .... me to buy a pen? ☐ 6

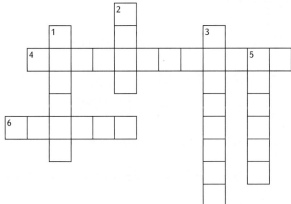

c Add a suffix to the word to make a noun. Sometimes
you need to change the spelling.

-ance	-er	-ion	-ist	-ity	-ment

1 win ....

2 enjoy ....

3 popular ....

4 educate ....

5 appear ....

6 design ....

7 final ....

8 entertain ....

9 attract .... ☐ 9

d Complete the sentences with the words in the box.

attention champion fashion museum
reality show star studio talent

1 I hate watching .... TV shows.

2 There are some wonderful paintings in the art ....

3 He loves all the media .... he gets!

4 She's a great singer – she's got a lot of natural
....

5 I was sitting in the .... audience for that show.

6 He practises a lot – he wants to be the world
.... one day!

7 She loves clothes. She wants to be a .... designer.

8 Would you ever go on a talent .... ?

9 He wants to become a famous sports .... ☐ 9

Correct it!

Correct these typical learner errors
from Units 5 and 6.

1 Parents let their children to have more freedom
than before.

....

2 We cant wear jeans.

....

3 We don't allowed to use mobile phones at school.

....

4 Do you allowed to take pets inside?

....

5 This book was write by J.K. Rowling.

....

6 Our exams will being finished soon.

....

7 He couldn't remember what just had happened.

....

8 The teacher gave me a higher note than before.

....

9 At the age of 15 I was allready in a band.

....

10 We took a lot of photos which will remember us of
the holiday.

....

GREEN: Great! Tell your teacher your score!

YELLOW: Not bad, but go to the website for extra practice.

RED: Talk to your teacher and look at Units 5 and 6
again. Go to the website for extra practice.

14	15	16	17	18	19	20	21	22	23	24	25	26	27	28	29	30

14	15	16	17	18	19	20	21	22	23	24	25	26	27	28	29	30

7 That's incredible!

Modal verbs of deduction: present
Modal verbs of deduction: past
Vocabulary: Extreme adjectives; Phrasal verbs with *go*
Interaction 7: Guessing what happened

1 Listen

a 🔊 **2.21** Look at the newspaper headlines and photos. What do you think the stories are about? Listen and check.

The real Harry Potter

Snake saves family

b 🔊 **2.21** Listen again. Are the sentences *right* (✓) or *wrong* (✗)? Correct the wrong sentences.

1 The real-life Harry Potter and the actor, Daniel Radcliffe, both have a scar.

2 People often think that the real-life Harry is lying about his name.

3 When he met his girlfriend, he had to show her his bus pass.

4 The Chinese man helped the snake because snakes are lucky.

5 He kept the snake as protection against wild animals.

6 The snake woke the man up by pulling his clothes with its teeth.

c Work with a partner. Answer the questions.

1 Do you think the stories are true? Why? / Why not?

2 Have you heard any strange stories in the news recently?

2 Vocabulary

Extreme adjectives

a 🔊 **2.22** Match the adjectives with the extreme adjectives. Then listen and check.

Adjective	Extreme adjective
1 cold	A tiny
2 big	B freezing
3 hungry	C huge
4 small	D starving
5 tired	E boiling
6 frightening	F awful
7 hot	G unbelievable
8 bad	H exhausted
9 surprising	I terrifying

> **Check it out!**
>
> ● Use *absolutely*, NOT *very* + extreme adjectives.
> He's **absolutely exhausted**.
> NOT ~~He's very exhausted~~.

b Complete the sentences with an extreme adjective from Exercise 2a.

1 Is dinner ready yet? I'm absolutely ....

2 It's .... in here. Can I close the window?

3 I'm .... ! It's 45°C in here!

4 Eight people can get in their car. It's absolutely ....

5 They've walked a long way today, so they'll probably be ....

6 My room's absolutely .... There's only space for one small bed.

7 We saw sharks when we were swimming. It was a .... experience!

8 The end of the film was .... ! I never thought he might be an alien!

c Work with a partner. Answer the questions.

1 What do you do when you are exhausted / boiling / starving / freezing?

2 When was the last time you saw or heard something unbelievable / terrifying / awful?

····▷ *When I'm starving I go out for a pizza.*

③ Grammar

Modal verbs of deduction: present

a Look at the examples. Then (circle) the correct words to complete the rules.

> ⟶ It **must be** really strange to have the same name as a character in a book.
> People **might not believe** that his name is really Harry Potter.
> It **can't be** there. I've just cleared out all the magazines from my room.
> It **may be** in that pile under the table.

- We use *might*, *may* or *could* when we think something in the present is **possible / impossible**.
- We use *must* when we are **certain / uncertain** that something is true.
- We use *can't* when we are certain that something is **possible / impossible**.
- Modal verbs **change / don't change** in the 3rd person (*he/she/it*).
- Modal verbs are followed by the **infinitive without *to* / -*ing* form**.

Grammar reference: Workbook page 92

Check it out!

- We do not use the negative *must not* for deductions. We can only use *can't*.
  Susie **can't be** at home now. I've just seen her in the park.
  NOT ~~Susie mustn't be at home now~~. I've just seen her in the park.

---

b (Circle) the correct words.

1 I don't really know what the answer is, but it *could / must* be 100.
2 The house is completely dark. Everybody *must / might* be out.
3 All that homework is for tomorrow? You *could / can't* be serious!
4 My sister *might / can't* be at home by now. She finished work early today.
5 I can't see the letters very well. They *can't / may* be an 'H' and a 'T'.
6 She *can't / might* come from Sweden. She doesn't speak Swedish.
7 He *might not / must* be at school today. He's got a bad cold.
8 I don't know whose phone it is – it *might / must* be Sammy's.

④ Speak

a Look at the pictures of strange things or events. Work with a partner. Use modal verbs of deduction to explain the pictures.

> ⟶ That can't be a real crocodile.
> ⟶ It must be a model of a crocodile. Maybe they are making a film.

b Work with another pair. Are your reactions and explanations the same?

c Read about two of the pictures, then explain your pictures to your partner.

Student A: Turn to page 124.
Student B: Turn to page 124.

⑤ Read and listen

a Look at the pictures. What do you think the story is about? Read the text and find out.

MOTHMAN

and the Men in Black

The bizarre events around the small town of Point Pleasant, West Virginia, started in November 1966. Four young people were going round an old factory outside the town when they noticed two red lights and stopped the car to investigate. They saw the shining, red eyes of a large animal. It was completely unlike any animal they had ever seen before. It was like a man, but bigger, with huge wings on its back. Terrified, they drove away as fast as they could and the creature went after them, flying at over 160km per hour!

Over the next few days, many more people said they had seen the creature. People began calling it Mothman. Other strange things went on in Point Pleasant. Unusual lights were seen in the sky and odd noises were heard. One woman was watching TV when she heard a strange buzzing noise outside. She went out and found Mothman hovering in the air about three metres away from her, so she immediately went back into the house. She was amazed when she discovered that her TV programme had ended. Somehow she had 'lost' about 25 minutes.

Many people thought Mothman must have come from outer space, but others thought the creature might be part of a government experiment. Then some strangers, dressed in black suits, arrived in town. They said they were government agents and visited people in their homes to warn them not to speak about Mothman in public. The townspeople were frightened of these 'Men in Black', and some thought they might have been extraterrestrials. They behaved very strangely, and some people said they didn't have any ears and they talked without moving their lips.

The people of Point Pleasant went through months of frightening events, then a terrible accident took place in December 1967. The main bridge in the town fell down and 46 people were killed. Mothman seemed to go away. Could there have been a connection between Mothman and the bridge accident?

Nine years later a journalist called Rick Moran decided to investigate the story. He thought the weird events may not have really happened. But nearly everyone he spoke to in Point Pleasant remembered what had happened clearly. Surely so many people can't have imagined Mothman?

Moran returned to New York and something very strange happened. His family and friends started to receive frightening phone calls; they were told to warn Moran not to speak or write about Point Pleasant. Were the messages from the Men in Black? Moran went on the radio and reported everything he knew, after which the warnings immediately stopped.

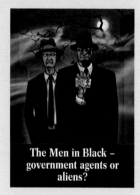

The Men in Black – government agents or aliens?

b 🔊 2.23 Read the text again and listen. Are the sentences *right* (✓), *wrong* (✗) or *doesn't say* (–)?

1 Mothman was first seen in Point Pleasant town centre.
2 The woman who 'lost' 25 minutes fell asleep in front of the TV.
3 Mothman was trying to attack and hurt people.
4 Some people thought the Men in Black were not human.
5 Mothman warned people about the bridge.
6 At first Rick Moran thought it was possible that the Mothman story was not true.
7 Some of Moran's friends tried to stop him from talking about Point Pleasant.

c Work with a partner. Answer the questions.

1 Do you think Mothman was real? Why? / Why not?
2 Who do you think the Men in Black were?
3 What films about monsters or aliens have you seen?

Culture Vulture

Did you know that in Britain, there are stories about the Loch Ness Monster, a strange creature that lives in a loch, or lake, in Scotland? Are there any stories about strange creatures in your country?

(6) Grammar

Modal verbs of deduction: past

a Look at the examples. Then (circle) the correct words to complete the rules.

> ⟶ *Some thought they **might have been** extraterrestrials.*
> *Many people thought Mothman **must have come** from outer space.*
> *Surely so many people **can't have imagined** Mothman?*
> *He thought the weird events **may not have** really **happened**.*

- We use *might/may/could have* when we think something is **possible** / **impossible** in the past.
- We use *must/can't have* when we are **certain** / **uncertain** about something in the past.
- We use modal verb + *have* + **past simple** / **past participle**.

Grammar reference: Workbook page 92

b Rewrite the sentences using a suitable modal verb. Sometimes more than one modal is possible.

1 I'm sure I didn't leave my keys in my room.
I can't have left my keys in my room .

2 Perhaps my brother ate the chocolates.
My brother ....

3 I am certain they were at the cinema yesterday.
They ....

4 Maybe we didn't lose the map on the train.
We ....

5 I'm sure he hasn't left without me.
He ....

c Work with a partner. Read the story, then guess what happened. Use past modals of deduction.

On 21 October 1978 Frederick Valentich, aged 20, took off in a small plane from Melbourne, Australia. 45 minutes later Frederick contacted the airport in Melbourne. He said he could see a huge aircraft flying very close to him. Later he said the plane seemed to be chasing him. Then, terrified, he spoke his final words to Melbourne: 'That strange aircraft is hovering on top of me again. It's hovering, and it's not an aircraft!' Frederick then disappeared. Rescue services looked for him but did not find anything. At the same time as the accident, about 20 people had seen a strange green light in the sky.

d 🔊 **2.24** Listen to four possible explanations of what might have happened. Are they the same as your explanations? Which is the most likely explanation?

(7) Pronunciation ⟨D·V·D⟩

Elision of *have*

a 🔊 **2.25** Listen to the pronunciation of the weak forms of *have* /əv/.

They could‿have seen an alien.
They must‿have been government agents.
He can't‿have been a vampire.

b 🔊 **2.26** Listen to the sentences. Write the number of times you hear the word *have* in each dialogue.

1 ☐   2 ☐   3 ☐   4 ☐

c 🔊 **2.26** Listen, check and repeat.

d Work with a partner. Take it in turns to say the sentences. Remember to use the weak form of *have* in the middle of the sentences.

1 You must have seen that light in the sky.
2 They could have forgotten to come.
3 It must have been a plane.
4 That noise could have been the cat.

(8) Vocabulary

Phrasal verbs with *go*

a Look at the sentences and <u>underline</u> the phrasal verbs with *go*.

1 Four young people were going round an old factory.
2 The creature went after them.
3 She went out and found Mothman hovering in the air.
4 She immediately went back into the house.

b 🔊 2.27 Match the phrasal verbs in the sentences with the definitions. Then listen and check.

> leave or disappear   continue   happen
> check   have an unpleasant or difficult experience

1 Strange things **went on** in Point Pleasant.
2 The mysterious events **went on** for so long.
3 They **went through** months of frightening events.
4 Mothman seemed to **go away**.
5 I always **go over** my work to look for mistakes.

c Replace the <u>underlined</u> words with the correct form of the phrasal verbs in Exercise 8b.

1 You should always <u>check</u> your homework before you give it to the teacher.
2 What's <u>happening</u> over there? What are all those people doing?
3 Silvia <u>had</u> a long illness last year but she's fine at the moment.
4 If this rain <u>continues</u>, we won't be able to play tennis.
5 There were some strange lights in the sky, then they <u>disappeared</u>.

d Work with a partner. Answer the questions.

1 What has been going on at your school recently?
2 If somebody took your money, would you go after them? Why? / Why not?
3 Do you know anyone who has been through a serious illness or another difficult experience?
4 How much time do you spend going over your homework before you hand it in?

Interaction 7 `DVD`

Guessing what happened

a 🔊 2.28 Listen to Sara and Darren trying to work out what happened yesterday evening. What do they think was strange? What do they think is the most likely explanation?

b 🔊 2.28 Listen again and match the sentence halves.

1 Maybe you're   A I think …
2 Actually,   B right, but …
3 I'm not   C must have happened.
4 Something   D sure about that.
5 That doesn't   E sound like Charlie.
6 I know what   F right.
7 You're probably   G might have happened.

c Work with a partner.

Student A: Turn to page 119.
Student B: Turn to page 122.

Portfolio 7

A mystery story

a In 1925 Percy Fawcett went into the jungle to find a lost city. Look at the pictures. What do you think might have happened to him?

b Read the story and put the paragraphs in the correct order.

A ☐ Three years later, George Dyott went to look for Fawcett and reported that he had died. Nobody believed him. Some people said Fawcett was a prisoner in a village, and others said that he was living happily in the city of 'Z'. Over the next 50 years about 100 adventurers may have died while they were looking for Fawcett's lost city.

B ☐ 1 Colonel Percy Fawcett was a British adventurer and the inspiration for Indiana Jones. He became famous in the early 1900s for his expeditions in the Amazon jungle in South America.

C ☐ In 1914 he discovered a South American tribe who told him about a beautiful city, hidden in the jungle. In 1925, he returned to Brazil to look for the city, which he called 'Z'. On May 25, Fawcett wrote to his wife saying that he and his son Jack were going to look for 'Z'. No one heard from them again.

D ☐ For years most archaeologists thought Fawcett had been crazy. But recently satellite cameras have found evidence of a huge, ancient city in the jungle. The city of 'Z' might have existed after all.

E ☐ At the beginning of the twentieth century, only native tribes were living in the Amazon jungle. It was full of dangerous insects, poisonous snakes and man-eating tribes. But Fawcett found the jungle mysterious and exciting.

c Which paragraph(s) …
1 introduce the main character?
2 give background details to the story?
3 describe the main events in the story?
4 describe recent events and conclude the story?

d Underline examples of these tenses in the story:
1 the past simple
2 the past continuous
3 the past perfect

e Which tense in Exercise d is used for …
1 the main events in a story?
2 something that happened before the main events?
3 the background to a story, or events going on for a period of time?

f Write a story about an unsolved mystery. Use one of the ideas in the box.

> a missing person   a strange creature
> an unsolved crime   a lost civilisation
> a UFO   an urban legend

g Read your partner's story. What do you think could have happened?

The Bahamas – myths and mysteries

An ideal place to surf, dive or just lie in the sun – the Bahamas is a modern holiday paradise. But there are many mysterious, ancient stories about the area. Here we try to separate the facts from the fantasy.

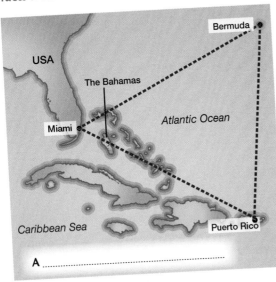

A ....

USA

Bermuda

The Bahamas

Miami

Atlantic Ocean

Caribbean Sea

Puerto Rico

The Bimini Road – part of Atlantis?

C ....

The myth
According to the Ancient Greek philosopher Plato, Atlantis was an island inhabited by a very advanced society, which suddenly vanished under the sea over 2,500 years ago. People used to think Atlantis was a mythical place, but recently some people have started to wonder whether it could have been real. One theory is that the Bimini Road, near Bimini Island in the Bahamas, is part of the lost capital of Atlantis.

The explanation
Many experts have investigated the Bimini Road and they say it can't have been a road or a wall. It is a natural rock formation.

The Bermuda Triangle

The myth
Hundreds of ships and planes have disappeared without a trace in the mysterious 'Bermuda Triangle', a huge area in the Atlantic Ocean. Many people think the incidents could be due to strange magnetic activity or extraterrestrial spaceships.

One of the most bizarre disappearances is that of 'Flight 19', five US Navy planes that vanished mysteriously. The rescue plane which went to look for them also disappeared. A total of 27 men were lost. Steven Spielberg included a fictional version of this story in his science-fiction film, *Close Encounters of the Third Kind*.

The explanation
The Flight 19 pilots thought they were flying over the Florida Keys, a group of islands near Miami, but they were actually over the Bahamas. They probably didn't have enough fuel to get back to land and they got lost far out at sea.

Most Bermuda Triangle accidents have probably been caused by extreme weather conditions. There are more hurricanes and unexpected storms in this area than in any other part of the Atlantic.

Chickcharnies

The myth
Chickcharnies live in the forests of Andros. They are half human, half bird with red eyes, three fingers, three toes and a tail, which they use to hang upside-down from trees. If you meet a chickcharnie and treat it with respect, you'll be lucky for the rest of your life. But if you are rude, your head will turn around completely!

The explanation
There once really was a bird like the Chickcharnie on Andros. It was a large three-toed owl that couldn't fly but could turn its head around a long way.

Lusca the sea monster

The myth
Lusca is a terrifying cross between a giant shark and an octopus, and attacks ships. This monster hides in 'blue holes', which are underwater cave systems between island lakes and the sea. Lusca is especially active around Andros, the largest island in the Bahamas, but it has been seen throughout the Caribbean Sea.

The explanation
Blue holes really *are* dangerous, but because of strong sea currents, not because of Lusca.

Mermaids

The myth
For centuries sailors have told stories about mermaids, creatures that are half woman and half fish. In 1616 an English captain, John Smith, noticed a woman swimming near the Bahamas. She had 'large eyes, rather too round, a finely shaped nose (a little too short) … and long green hair'. Suddenly she rolled over and he saw she had a fish's tail. People still believe that a mermaid lives in Mermaid Hole, a lake on Cat Island in the Bahamas.

The explanation
Many people think that mermaids must have been manatees, large sea mammals which can be up to four metres long. These friendly, curious animals often approach ships. At night they just *might* look like mermaids.

B ....

1 Culture World: The Bahamas

a Do you know any strange myths or mysteries? What happened?

b Read the magazine article quickly and match the captions with the pictures.

1 Is this part of a lost city?

2 Sociable manatees coming to say 'hello'.

3 Why is this area of sea so dangerous?

c Read the text again and answer the questions.

1 What three sports activities can you do in the Bahamas?

2 What do many people think causes the strange disappearances in the Bermuda Triangle?

3 How many planes disappeared in the Flight 19 incident?

4 What is the most probable reason for the Bermuda Triangle disappearances?

5 Why should you be polite to a Chickcharnie?

6 What do the experts think about the Bimini Road?

7 What are 'blue holes'?

8 What did John Smith think he saw at first? What did he think he saw later?

d Find the words in the text that mean ...

1 disappeared suddenly (Bermuda Triangle)

2 politeness towards someone/something (Chickcharnies)

3 live in a place (Bimini Road)

4 ask yourself questions about something (Bimini Road)

5 a mixture of two different things (Lusca)

6 see or be aware of something (Mermaids)

e Work with a partner. Answer the questions.

1 Do you believe the explanations of the mysteries? Why? / Why not?

2 Do you think some mysteries are impossible to explain? Why? / Why not?

2 Your project

Mysteries in your country

a Work in a group. Complete a table about your country with information about a popular mystery and some possible explanations.

Place	Cat Island
Mystery	A mermaid (half woman, half fish) still lives in Mermaid Hole
Explanation	People might have seen manatees and thought they were human

b Write an article about the mystery and the explanations. Use the information in Exercise 2a. Include:

- a title and sub-headings
- details about the mystery
- possible explanations
- photos and captions

THE ROSWELL UFO

Over 60 years after the accident in Roswell, nobody agrees on what really happened. We try to uncover the truth.

In June or July 1947, an unidentified flying object (UFO) crashed in the city of Roswell, New Mexico in the United States. The event was quickly forgotten until 1978 when Major Jesse Marcel was interviewed about the accident.

After conducting hundreds of interviews, a group of researchers came to the conclusion that an alien aircraft had crashed close to Roswell. Several books have been written on the subject. But what happened exactly? Was it an alien spaceship? Or a weather balloon? Or debris coming from a top secret government experiment designed by the United States in order to test the possibility of detecting Russian nuclear tests and missiles with equipment on high altitude balloons? One thing is certain - the mystery has only got thicker.

UFO CRASH SITE

8 Gaming and gadgets

Quantifiers review
Non-defining relative clauses
Vocabulary: Health problems; Technology
Interaction 8: Asking for and giving explanations

1 Read and listen

a Look at the two pictures. Which do you think is the healthier activity? Which do you think is more fun?

(1) Scientists at the University of Oklahoma have found that playing active video games can be as effective for teenagers as doing moderate exercise. The research shows that active video games can help to keep you fit. This is especially important for many young people of today's generation who often spend too much time watching television or playing games sitting down.

Dr Kevin Short believes that too many young people don't do enough exercise, and although playing active video games is no substitute for 'real' sports activities, you can burn calories. He thinks that any exercise is better than no exercise at all.

The investigation tested teenagers while they watched television and played active video games. Compared to watching television, the calories burned while active gaming increased by two or three times.

Overall, the energy used while playing active video games was similar to walking quite fast. So, for young people who play a lot of computer games, changing to physically active games can be a safe, fun and valuable means of doing exercise.

(2) Active video games can play an important role in getting young people off the sofa and interested in physical activity. But are they really a replacement for traditional exercise? Colleen Greene, MA, from the University of Michigan, doesn't think so.

In recent research, she found that some video games, like golf or tennis, require as little activity as a swing of the wrist. This is not enough to qualify as 'real' exercise. Research shows that although you can burn real calories during virtual gaming, if you played the game or sport in 'real life' you would burn three to four times the amount.

Greene does note, however, that a few active video games can help to improve confidence and hand–eye co-ordination. She believes that for some teenagers active gaming can be a safe place to try a new sport, which they may then want to actually play. She is sure, though, that it is not enough exercise to just play video games. She suggests that young people should get outside in the fresh air and give 'real' sports a try.

b Student A: Read text 1. Student B: Read text 2. Answer the questions about your text.

1 What positive points of active gaming are mentioned in your text?

2 What negative points of active gaming are mentioned?

3 How does your text compare active gaming to real exercise?

4 In general, is the article in favour of active gaming? Why? / Why not?

c Work with your partner. Tell him/her about your article.

d 🔊 **2.29** Read and listen to both texts and answer the questions.

1 Have you ever played any active video games? If so, which ones?

2 Do you think active video gaming is a good way to keep fit? Why? / Why not?

3 Which text makes a stronger argument? Which text do you agree with most? Why?

Culture Vulture

Did you know that British people spend about £4 billion a year on computer games and consoles? Do people in your country spend more money on gaming, music or films? What about you?

② Vocabulary

Health problems

a 🔊 **2.30** Match the phrases with the pictures. Then listen and check.

> **1** He's got a headache. **2** He's got flu.
> **3** She's got a cold. **4** She's got a cough.
> **5** She's got a sore throat.
> **6** He's got a temperature.
> **7** She feels dizzy. **8** He feels sick.
> **9** She's got a pain in her chest.
> **10** His wrist hurts.

> **Check it out!**
>
> ● We use different words to talk about pain:
> *sore* (adjective): I've got a **sore** knee.
> *pain* (noun): I've got a **pain** in my foot.
> *hurt* (verb): My wrists **hurt**.
> *ache* (noun): I've got a **headache**.
> *ache* (verb): My arms **ache**.

b (Circle) the correct words.

1 We danced for hours yesterday and today my legs *pain / ache*.

2 I've got a *hurt / pain* in my arm.

3 He's been eating junk food all day and now he's got a stomach *sore / ache*.

4 The world is going round and round, I feel quite *dizzy / sore*.

5 My feet *hurt / pain*!

6 I've got a *sore / hurt* arm from too much active gaming.

c Do you know any more words about health? Write them down.

d Work with a partner. Answer the questions.

1 When was the last time you had flu or a temperature?

2 What do you do when you have a bad cold or flu?

3 When was the last time your body ached from doing lots of exercise?

4 What health problems do you think active gaming can give you?

③ Pronunciation 📀

Words with *ough*

a 🔊 **2.31** The letters *ough* can be pronounced in different ways. Listen to these words.

> /ɒf/ cough /ʌf / enough
> /uː/ through /əʊ/ although

b 🔊 **2.32** (Circle) the word in each group that doesn't have the same pronunciation. Then listen and check.

1 although through though

2 cough true off

3 rough now tough

4 new through cough

5 enough tough through

c 🔊 **2.33** Listen and write the word from Exercise 3b that you hear in each sentence.

1 .... **4** ....

2 .... **5** ....

3 .... **6** ....

d 🔊 **2.34** Listen and repeat.

> *Although he saw him clearly enough through the window, he was too tough to catch!*

4 Grammar

Quantifiers review

Check it out!
- Adjectives come before *enough*, but after *too*.
  It's **too** big.   It's big **enough**.
  It's **not** big **enough**. NOT ~~It's not enough big~~.

a Look at the examples. Then (circle) the correct words to complete the rules.

⋯⋯⟩ *Children spend **too much time** watching television.*
***Too many children** don't do enough exercise.*
*Playing games doesn't give you **enough exercise**.*
***A few** active video games can help to improve confidence.*
***Fewer girls** play video games than boys.*
*I have **less time** for gaming than when I was younger.*

- We use **enough** / **too much** to mean 'the right quantity', and **too many** / **not enough** to mean 'less than the right quantity'.

- We use *too much* and *too many* to mean **more** / **less** than the right quantity.
- We use *less* and *fewer* to mean a **larger** / **smaller** quantity.
- We use *a few* to refer to a **small** / **large** quantity.
- *Quantifiers* always come **before** / **after** the noun.
- We use *too much* and *less* with **uncountable** / **countable** nouns.
- We use *too many*, *fewer* and *a few* with **uncountable** / **countable** nouns.

Grammar reference: Workbook page 94

b Complete the sentences with the correct quantifier.

1 I haven't got .... money to buy the game and the remote control.
2 .... students always arrive late to class, but most arrive on time.
3 I think we've got .... homework! I'll never have time to do it all tonight!
4 There were .... people at the party – I couldn't get in the room!
5 You're .... fast .... to be good at gaming.
6 I watch .... films than I used to as I haven't got much free time these days.

c Complete the second sentence with the correct quantifier so that it means the same as the first sentence.

1 He's got so many clothes he doesn't have time to wear them all!
He's got .... clothes.
2 She needs more free time.
She hasn't got .... free time.
3 On Wednesday there were 28 students but today there are only 19.
There are .... students here today than on Wednesday.
4 I used to watch a lot of TV when I was younger but now I don't.
I watch .... TV now.
5 There are only two or three video games that I enjoy.
I only enjoy .... video games.

5 Speak

a Work with a partner. Use the words in the circles to talk about your opinions.

① I think there are ...
I think there's ...
I've got / I haven't got ...
There are ...
There's ...
I've spent ...

② too many ...
too much ...
not enough ...
enough ...
a few ...
fewer ...
less ...

③ time ...
money ...
people ...
homework ...
... on TV.
... on the internet.
women ...
men ...

There are fewer women video game designers than men.

I haven't got enough free time to do sport.

6 Vocabulary

Technology

a 🔊 **2.35** Match the words with the definitions. Then listen and check.

1 games console ☐
2 GPS (global positioning system) ☐
3 run out of battery ☐
4 plug in ☐
5 touch screen ☐
6 voice-activated ☐
7 cable ☐
8 memory card ☐

A operated by speaking
B have no power
C a plastic-covered wire
D a machine with controls that you use for playing video games
E using satellites to show your exact position
F connect to electricity so the gadget works
G a small, portable disc drive for storing information
H operated with your hands, not a keyboard

b Complete the sentences with words from Exercise 6a.

1 I store my photos on a
....

2 My brother has just bought a
.... for his car so he won't get lost.

3 I can't call you – my mobile phone has
....

4 We won't need keyboards when all computers are ....

5 Every gadget comes with its own .... to recharge it.

6 He's got the latest .... so he can play some brilliant games.

c Do you know any more technology words? Write them down.

d Work in a group. Answer the questions.

1 Which objects do you have that you have to plug in?

2 When was the last time that something you own ran out of battery at a bad moment?

3 When was the last time you downloaded something from the internet?

4 Do you think that GPS is useful? Why? / Why not?

7 Listen

a 🔊 **2.36** Listen to a podcast from 'Technology Today'. Match the gadgets with the extreme sports.

b 🔊 **2.36** Listen again. Choose the correct answer: A, B or C.

1 The heated jacket comes with ...
   A a place to recharge an MP3 player.
   B a free MP3 player.
   C a pocket to keep a battery in.

2 For the jacket to work, you must ...
   A put batteries in your pocket.
   B plug it in the night before.
   C take your laptop with you.

3 The software for the GPS tracker ...
   A isn't necessary to use the gadget.
   B has to be bought online.
   C is free if you buy the gadget.

4 The GPS tracker ...
   A is linked to a website.
   B counts the number of kilometres cycled.
   C sends a message to emergency services if you have an accident.

5 The waterproof camera ...
   A is attached to the surfboard.
   B is attached to a helmet.
   C is hand-held.

6 The camera can film for ...
   A four hours.
   B five hours.
   C six hours.

c Work in a group. Answer the questions.

1 Which of the gadgets do you think is the best? Why?

2 Have you ever listened to a podcast like this? What was it about?

3 Have you done any of the sports that Pete tried? Which ones?

(8) Grammar

Non-defining relative clauses

a Look at the examples. Then (circle) the correct words to complete the rules.

> ⋯➤ *It's a heated jacket, **which** isn't so new, but this one has a really special feature.*
> *This week Pete, **who** is our very own 'Gadget Guru', has tested three gadgets.*
> *My mate Jack, **whose** brother is a pro-biker, has already got one of these and loves it.*
> *I went to the southwest coast, **where** the waves were huge, for a bit of surfing.*

- In non-defining relative clauses we use commas around the clause.
- Non-defining relative clauses give us **extra information / essential information**.
- We use *which* for **people / things / places**.
- We use *who* for **people / things / places**.
- We use **whose / who** instead of *his*, *her* or *their*.
- We use *where* for **people / things / places**.

Grammar reference: Workbook page 94

Check it out!

- We don't use *that* in non-defining relative clauses:
  His house, **which** is the biggest in the city, cost over a million euros.
  NOT ~~His house, that is the biggest in the city, cost over a million euros.~~

b Put commas in the correct places to make non-defining relative clauses.

1 The high-speed train which is new this year was designed in Japan.
2 My home town where I was born and grew up is famous for its beautiful beaches.
3 My friend Josh whose parents are both politicians wants to be an actor.
4 His computer which he only bought last week has already got a virus.

c Make one sentence from two.

1 Cathy is such a computer addict. (She's my sister's best friend.)
   Cathy, who's my sister's best friend, is such a computer addict.
2 My phone has broken already. (It cost £150!)
3 This laptop picks up a wifi signal at the top of a mountain. (It's small enough to fit in my pocket.)
4 Jack is really bad at biology. (His parents are both doctors.)
5 Footballers earn far too much money. (Their job is really easy and fun.)
6 My new webcam has a built-in microphone. (I got it for my birthday.)

d Complete the sentences so they are true for you.

1 One of my favourite actors, who I really admire, is ....
2 My favourite gadget, which I often use, is ....
3 A special place, where I'd like to be right now, is ....

Interaction 8 (DVD)

Asking for and giving explanations

a 🔊 **2.37** Listen to the conversation between Hattie and her grandma. Tick (✓) the gadget her grandma has.

a high-visibility walking stick

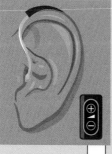
a remote-control hearing aid

reading glasses with built-in lights

b 🔊 **2.37** Listen again. Who says the phrases, Grandma (*G*) or Hattie (*H*)?

1 Sort of. ☐
2 I've got no idea what a ZX2000-and-whatever console is. ☐
3 Oh, I see. ☐
4 How does it work? ☐
5 I don't know what that is! ☐
6 What happens if you press this button? ☐
7 If you press that … ☐

c Work with a partner.
   Student A: Turn to page 119.
   Student B: Turn to page 122.

Portfolio 8

A formal letter of complaint

a Read the letter. How many complaints does Pablo have about the camera he bought?

16A Station Road
Longfield
Birmingham
BM4 7XY

Dear Sir or Madam,

I am writing to complain about the 'MiniDigi 75 x-sport video camera' I bought from your website in February. I am usually very happy with your products, but this time I am very disappointed.

Your site informed me that the camera would take 3–5 days to arrive. I placed my order on the 7th and eventually received my camera on the 23rd after making five phone calls to your customer service number. When the camera arrived, I was disappointed to discover that the box didn't contain the camera bag that was included in the price. In addition to this, the battery does not work properly. I followed the instructions for recharging the battery, but instead of the advertised 9-hour battery life, the camera only lasts for 5 hours before it needs to be recharged. This is very inconvenient because I bought the camera to film skating competitions, which often last all day. I am also very disappointed with the quality of the picture. It should be 8 mega-pixels and HD but I'm afraid that the quality is not good enough. Please find enclosed a photo taken with this camera.

To resolve the problem, I suggest that you send me the camera bag immediately and I would also like you to change the camera for a different model. I would like the MiniDigi 82 instead, for the same price.

I would like a solution to my problem within the next week. I look forward to hearing from you soon.

Yours faithfully,
Pablo Baker.

b Read the letter again and match paragraphs 1–4 with the information.

offers an idea for a possible solution ☐   finishes the letter ☐

says where and when the item was bought ☐   gives details about the problems with the item ☐

c Look at these phrases from the letter. Put them into the correct column in the table.

A I am writing to complain about …
B I was disappointed to discover that …
C In addition to this,
D This is very inconvenient because …
E I am also very disappointed with the quality …
F To resolve the problem, I suggest that you …
G I would like a solution to my problem …
H I look forward to hearing from you soon.

Reason for writing	Problems	Solutions	Other useful phrases

d Write a letter to complain about one of the following products. Use formal language and the phrases in Exercise c to help you.

1 an MP3 player that doesn't work well
2 a laptop which has very short battery life
3 a camera helmet that doesn't fit you
4 something else you choose

e Work with a partner. Read your partner's letter. Do you think the company would offer a solution? Why? / Why not?

ZEROES AND ONES

1 Song

a 🔊 **2.38** Listen to the first verse of the song. What does 'zeroes and ones' refer to?

A large amounts of money

B 'bits' and 'bytes' used for computer programming

C an important date in history

b 🔊 **2.39** Listen to the whole song and put the verses in the correct order.

☐ **¹ This time the revolution will be computerised**

You'll know it as you do it in real time before your eyes

Slip between realities

² There's more to this than anything that you or I can see

The world is mine the world is yours and here's the cause

Zeroes and ones will take us there

Zeroes and ones will take us there

☐ **³ This time, we've split the world once more**
⁴ There's those that have and those that don't in information wars

We're not alone 'cause all is known and it's everywhere

It's everywhere

Zeroes and ones will take us there

Zeroes and ones will take us there

Zeroes and ones will take us there

☐ **⁵ Across the world the message flies, information, truth and lies**
⁶ It's all yours and it's all mine, you just have to find the time

We're all the same, we share the blame, we play the games

If it's yes or no the decision is easy, it's easy

Zeroes and ones will take us there

Zeroes and ones will take us there

☐ I've stared into the heart of it all

Seen the pictures on the wall

The beat of a heart

The oceans part and the patterns in my mind

c 🔊 **2.39** Listen to the song again and check.

d Read the song lyrics and match the lines in **bold** to their meanings.

A Computers are going to play an important role in world changes. ☐

B The only limit to what you can do online is the time you have available. ☐

C Now the planet is divided in two. ☐

D Online communication is fast, but the information isn't always honest. ☐

E There's a big gap between people who have access to technology and people who don't. ☐

F You and I will never fully understand technology. ☐

e Work in a group. Answer the questions.

1 Do you agree that the world is divided into people who have computers and access to the internet and those who don't? Why? / Why not?

2 How do you think computers are going to affect people's lives in the future?

3 In what ways was daily life different before computers and the internet were invented?

(2) Sound check

a ◁))) **2.40** Listen to the chorus of the song and focus on the words that are clearly linked together. Choose the correct option.

1 zeroes_and ones will take_us there

2 zeroes and ones will_take us_there

b ◁))) **2.41** Listen to these lines from the song. Draw lines to show where the words are linked.

1 It's all yours and it's all mine

2 If it's yes or no the decision is easy, it's easy

3 The world is mine the world is yours and here's the cause

4 I've stared into the heart of it all

c ◁))) **2.41** Listen again and repeat.

Jesus Jones

(3) Musical notes

Electronic music

a ◁))) **2.42** Listen to some different kinds of electronic music. Write the correct decade for each extract.

1 .... 2 ....

3 ....

b Do you like electronic music? Why? / Why not? How do you think music will change in the future?

1960s

1980s

1990s

ELECTRONIC MUSIC

The song *Zeroes and Ones* was recorded in 1993 by the band Jesus Jones.

Electronic music started in the 1960s. The first 'sound synthesisers' looked like computers. The strange-sounding music they produced was used as background music in films and TV programmes, especially for science-fiction programmes. In the 1970s and '80s, bands started using electronic keyboards along with more traditional instruments. The keyboards could create interesting sounds and rhythms. In the 1990s and 2000s, electronic dance music became popular. Live bands were often replaced by DJs, who 'mixed' the music on stage.

Review ⑦ and ⑧

① Grammar

a Kate and Sara are at a party on Saturday. Match 1–4 with A–D to make Sara's possible answers.

Kate: There's somebody at the door. Do you think it's Jake?

Sara:

1 It must be Jake. ☐

2 It could be Jake. ☐

3 It can't be Jake. ☐

4 It might not be Jake. ☐

A He said he was going away for the weekend.

B He said he probably wouldn't have time to come.

C He said he would come at this time.

D He said he would come if he had time. ☐ 4

b (Circle) the correct words.

1 Their car isn't there. They *must / can't* have gone away.

2 He *might not / may* have seen us, but I'm not sure.

3 She *might / can't* have forgotten the box. I left it where she would see it.

4 I don't know what that noise was. It *could / must* have been a mouse.

5 Hurry up! The concert *might not / may* have already started.

6 He beat me at the game. He *can't / must* have practised it a lot.

7 They only left a few minutes ago. They *can't / must* have arrived yet! ☐ 7

c Complete the sentences with the words in the box.

| a few   enough   fewer   less |
| not enough   too many   too much |

1 Have you got .... food for your lunch? Do you want some fruit?

2 We've got .... minutes before the film starts. Let's get a drink.

3 There's .... time to play the video game. It takes a long time.

4 I can't come to the party, I've got .... homework.

5 You've given me .... ice cream than him! Can I have some more?

6 I tried to get tickets, but there were .... people in the queue in front of me.

7 There were .... people at the match today than there were last week. ☐ 7

d Join the two sentences using non-defining relative clauses.

1 Her laptop has got a huge memory. It was really expensive.

....

2 Brighton is a great place for live music. I used to live there.

....

3 My cousin is coming to stay with us. He works in South Korea.

....

4 Lena is going to be in our basketball team. Her sister is in my class.

....

5 These trainers are the best I've ever had. I got them in Paris.

....

6 The Blue Door Café is my favourite place to meet friends. It's in Main Street.

.... ☐ 6

e Complete the second sentence so that it means the same as the first.

1 It's possible that he's Johnny Depp.
.... Johnny Depp.

2 I need more money to buy those jeans.
I haven't .... to buy those jeans.

3 I'm sure that the answer isn't 50.
The answer .... 50.

4 There are more boys than girls in my class.
There .... than boys in my class.

5 It might be time to go in.
Perhaps .... to go in.

6 It was definitely a wolf.
It .... been a wolf. ☐ 6

How are you doing?

How many points have you got? Put two crosses on the chart: one for grammar and one for vocabulary.

	1	2	3	4	5	6	7	8	9	10	11	12	13
Grammar													

	1	2	3	4	5	6	7	8	9	10	11	12	13
Vocabulary													

② Vocabulary

a Replace the adjectives in **bold** with extreme adjectives.

1 Turn on the heating, it's **cold** .... in here.
2 I can't wait for dinner, I'm **hungry** .... !
3 We watched a **frightening** .... film, and afterwards I couldn't sleep.
4 When they got to the top of the mountain, they were **tired** .... !
5 Have you seen their new puppy? It's **small** .... !
6 It was **hot** .... , so we swam every day.
7 They've got a **big** .... garden with a swimming pool.
8 I got ten out of ten in Maths! That's **surprising** .... !
9 That was a really **bad** .... film!

☐ 9

b Circle the correct words.

1 I could see that something strange was going *off / on*.
2 Going *round / after* the factory was very interesting.
3 I went *out / away* into the garden.
4 My mum offered to go *round / over* my work for me.
5 We went *through / over* a very difficult time.
6 I shouted at him and he went *after / away*.
7 I called to her, but she went *on / over* walking.

☐ 7

c Complete the sentences with the words in the box.

ache feel got hurts pain sore

1 I've got a .... leg.
2 He's got a terrible head............................ .
3 I .... sick after eating all that chocolate!
4 Have you .... a cough?
5 I've got a .... in my chest.
6 Oh, my back .... !

☐ 6

d Put the letters in the correct order and make technology words.

1 mmeroy racd ....
2 glup ni ....
3 mages noclose ....
4 blaec ....
5 tchou creens ....
6 vioec-tacivtaed ....
7 PGS ....
8 rnu tuo fo abttrey ....

☐ 8

Correct it!

Correct these typical learner errors from Units 7 and 8.

1 There was news about the terryfing accident that morning.
   ....
2 We went to Ginza, where is in the centre of Tokyo.
   ....
3 There isn't enought space for another bed.
   ....
4 There was fewer traffic on the roads.
   ....
5 She hurted her shoulder.
   ....
6 It maybe dangerous, but it would be exciting.
   ....
7 We shouldn't eat too much oily dishes.
   ....
8 People should use a bicycle, wich is less expensive than a car.
   ....
9 My stomack hurt after eating the seafood.
   ....
10 They had to much free time, with nothing to do.
   ....

9 Seeing is believing

as if, *as though* and *like*
a/an, *the* or no article
Vocabulary: Adjectives of opinion; Truth and lies
Interaction 9: Being tactful

1 Listen

a Work in a group. Answer the questions.

1 What type of art do/don't you like? Why?
2 Have you ever been to an art or photography exhibition? What did you see?

b 🔊 **3.2** Listen to two people talking about the pictures. Tick (✓) the adjectives you hear.

amusing ☐	annoying ☐	depressing ☐
shocking ☐	hideous ☐	upsetting ☐
confusing ☐	gorgeous ☐	impressive ☐
fascinating ☐		

c 🔊 **3.2** Listen again. Are the sentences *right* (✓) or *wrong* (✗)? Correct the wrong sentences.

1 One of the speakers doesn't understand picture A.
2 Both speakers like picture B.
3 One speaker prefers picture C to Picasso's art.
4 Both speakers are impressed by picture E.

2 Vocabulary

Adjectives of opinion

a 🔊 **3.3** Match the adjectives in Exercise 1b with the definitions. Then listen and check.

A making you laugh ....
B very beautiful or attractive ....
C extremely interesting ....
D making you feel a little angry ....
E making you feel unhappy and worried ....
F really ugly or horrible ....
G very good ....
H making you feel very sad ....
I difficult to understand ....
J very surprising and horrible ....

b Circle the correct adjectives.

1 It's a very *confusing / amusing* film. It makes me laugh.
2 He finds that singer *fascinating / shocking*. He watches her videos every day.
3 I hate that dress! It's *gorgeous / hideous*!
4 I can't understand this – it's so *impressive / confusing*.
5 This cold, wet weather is really *depressing / gorgeous*.

③ Grammar

as if, *as though* and *like*

a Look at the examples. Then ⟨circle⟩ the correct words to complete the rules.

> ┄┄▷ It feels **as though** the lines are moving, but they're not.
> It looks **as if** a face is looking out of the picture.
> The hands look **like** they're holding a child.
> It's **like** a Picasso painting.
> I love optical illusions **like** this.
> It's **like** looking at a child's painting.

- We use *as if/though* or *like* to describe how a situation **really is / seems to be**.
- We can use *like* to say something is **different from / similar to** something else.
- *As if* and *as though* are followed by a clause with a subject + a verb.
- *Like* can be followed by a clause, but this use is **formal / informal**.
- *Like* is usually followed by a noun, pronoun or *-ing* form.

Grammar reference: Workbook page 96

Check it out!

- *As if*, *as though* and *like* are often used with verbs of sensation: *look, seem, feel, sound, taste*.
  It **feels as if** we're moving.
  This song **sounds like** the last one.

---

b ⟨Circle⟩ the correct words. Sometimes both answers are possible.

1 It sounds *like / as if* an aircraft.
2 He loves going to art exhibitions. He's *as though / like* an art critic.
3 The photos you sent us are beautiful. They look *as if / like* a professional photographer took them.
4 It looks *as though / like* it's going to rain.
5 You look *as / like* your sister.
6 These singers sounded *like / as if* professionals.
7 My ankle feels *as if / as though* it might be broken.

c Work with a partner. Complete the sentences so they are true for you, then compare.

1 I feel as if life is perfect when …
2 People sometimes say I look like …
3 When I hear my favourite song, I feel as though …
4 I want to be more like …

④ Speak

a Look at the photos. Decide which look real and which look as though they have been changed using a computer.

b Work with a partner. Compare your opinions about the photos.

A: *I think photo A could be real. It looks like my grandmother's cat.*

B: *I think it's fake. It looks as though someone's changed the eye colour with a computer.*

c Check your answers on page 124. How many did you guess correctly?

5 Read and listen

a What type of images are used in adverts to sell these products?

> beauty products   cars
> food   holidays   technology

b Read the text quickly and (circle) the products in Exercise 5a that are mentioned in the text.

c 🔊 **3.4** Read the text again and listen. Choose the correct answer: A, B or C.

1 In the past, editing photos was … than it is today.
   A easier
   B more difficult
   C more common

2 Today, most people use photo-editing software to …
   A create strange images.
   B create professional photos.
   C change their own photos.

3 The writer thinks that many people …
   A have bad hair and bad skin.
   B feel happy with their body image.
   C like seeing perfect pictures of famous people.

4 The writer asks … in adverts.
   A if it is OK to lie
   B when the camera doesn't lie
   C why the camera lies

d Work in a group. Answer the questions.

1 Do you sometimes alter the appearance of your photos? Why? / Why not?

2 Should companies change people's appearance in adverts? Why? / Why not?

Culture Vulture

One beauty company found that only 12% of women are 'very satisfied' with their appearance. They also found that 68% 'strongly agree' that the images of beauty shown in the media are unrealistic. Do you think the media makes people feel bad about themselves? Is it a good idea to use ordinary people in advertising campaigns?

The camera never lies

We have all heard the expression 'The camera never lies', but is this really true? Everywhere we look we see photos of gorgeous people with amazingly perfect smiles, or mouth-watering images of food that looks too good to eat. However, are these photos real, or are they fake?

IN THE PAST, only professional photographers were able to change the appearance of a photo, but nowadays people can adapt their own images at home with a computer and photo-editing software. It seems as though there are no longer any photos of people with red eyes or spots because more and more of us are editing our own pictures. As well as changing eye colour, we can copy and paste someone into a different situation or add special effects to the photo. We can change people's physical appearance – they can become prettier, slimmer, taller or even uglier, fatter and older!

The power of photo editing.

Most of us would be shocked if we realised how much the beauty industry depends on photo manipulation. Almost all images used to sell beauty products are altered to make the models look younger or more beautiful. Perhaps if we saw the original photo, we wouldn't worry so much about our own appearance. One beauty company ran a campaign to tell the truth behind photo manipulation in advertising. They wanted the campaign to make people aware of natural beauty.

But if we are truthful, how many of us want to open a magazine to find unedited photos of supermodels with bad skin or having a bad hair day? Perhaps we prefer the magazine to be full of these 'perfect' fake images. So maybe the question we need to ask is not 'Does the camera ever lie?', but 'Should advertisements use real pictures and tell the truth about their products?'

6 Grammar

a/an, the or no article

a Look at the examples. Then (circle) the correct words to complete the rules.

> ⤑ *Have you been sent **an amusing photo**?*
> *One beauty company ran **a campaign** …*
> *They wanted **the campaign** to make people aware …*
> ***The beauty industry** depends on photo manipulation a lot.*
> ***Images** are altered to make the models look younger.*
> *People can adapt their own images **at home**.*

- *A/An* means **one of many / the only one**.
- *The* means **one of many / the only one**.
- We use *a / the* with someone or something that we mention for the first time.
- We use *a / the* with someone or something that we know about or is already mentioned.
- We use *the / no article* to talk about plural and uncountable nouns in general.
- We use **no article / the** with some places (school, work, university, home, bed).

Grammar reference:
Workbook page 96

b (Circle) the correct words.

1 Do you like taking *a / the / –* photos? Why? / Why not?
2 Have you been to *an / the / –* art exhibition? Where?
3 Do you like *a / the / –* dogs? Why? / Why not?
4 Have you done *a / the / –* homework you got last week?
5 Would you like to get *a / the / –* job or go to *a / the / –* university when you leave *a / the / –* school? Why?

c Work with a partner. Answer the questions in Exercise 6b.

d Complete the text with *a/an* or *the* or leave the space blank where no article is needed.

The human camera

Steven Wiltshire is known as the 'human camera' because he has [1]............ photographic memory.

His teachers noticed his amazing memory while he was at [2]............ school. Now, he is [3]............ incredible artist who is able to draw [4]............ whole city from memory. His memory is so good that he draws [5]............ exact number of windows in each building. In 2008 he went on [6]............ short helicopter ride over [7]............ city of London looking at all [8]............ buildings along [9]............ River Thames. After [10]............ helicopter ride he drew [11]............ panoramic view of [12]............ city. He has also drawn [13]............ other cities including [14]............ Rome, Madrid and Tokyo.

7 Pronunciation 🔘DVD

The sounds /ð/ and /θ/

a 🔊 3.5 There are two ways to say *th* – /ð/ and /θ/. Listen to the examples.

/ð/ **th**e, **th**ough, bro**th**er   /θ/ tru**th**, **th**ink, nor**th**

b 🔊 3.6 Write the words in the correct column. Then listen and check.

~~there~~ ~~thing~~ birthday month
sunbathing they truthful with

ð	θ
there	thing

c 🔊 3.7 (Circle) the word with a different pronunciation of *th*. Then listen, check and repeat.

1 though	through	three	mouth
2 athletics	bath	rather	thin
3 their	together	other	thank
4 throw	teeth	mother	maths
5 theatre	although	thumb	tooth
6 south	these	then	weather
7 clothes	that	length	this

(8) Vocabulary Truth and lies

a 🔊 **3.8** Match the words in **bold** with the definitions. Then listen and check.

1 Why do you tell **lies** all the time? No one ever believes anything you say.

2 You can believe him completely. He always tells **the truth**.

3 I think advertising companies should be more **truthful** about their products.

4 They tried to use **fake** passports to get into the country.

5 This advert uses a special camera **trick** to make the food look perfect.

6 Adverts **fool** us because models look more beautiful than they really are.

7 I told a **white lie** and said that her cake was delicious, but between you and me, it was overcooked!

8 He **forged** a famous artist's signature on his painting.

A the true facts about something (noun)

B make an illegal or false copy of something, like a document (verb)

C things that are not true (noun)

D make someone believe something that is not true (verb)

E not real, but made to look real (adj)

F honest (adj)

G something that makes things look different from how they really are (noun)

H a lie that someone tells in order to be polite or to avoid upsetting someone (noun)

b Complete the sentences with words in Exercise 8a.

1 Don't tell .... ! I want to know what really happened!

2 Beauty companies use camera .... in their adverts.

3 They're not real diamonds. They're ....

4 I want you to tell me the .... and explain what really happened.

5 Don't let adverts .... you into thinking that something is perfect.

c Work with a partner. Answer the questions.

1 Is a fake suntan better than a real suntan? Why? / Why not?

2 Has anyone ever fooled you? What happened?

3 When did you last tell a white lie? Why?

Check it out!

- We *tell the truth* and *tell lies*.
  She always **tells the truth**. NOT ~~She always says the truth.~~
  You mustn't **tell lies**. NOT ~~You mustn't say lies~~.

Culture Vulture

Did you know that in Britain 500,000 fake bank notes are found each year? If you find one, you should take it to a bank and hand it in.

Interaction 9 Being tactful

a 🔊 **3.9** Listen to two conversations with Lindsay. Who tells white lies to be tactful about Lindsay's jeans, Robyn or Jen?

b 🔊 **3.10** Listen again to conversation two. Number the phrases Jen says in the order you hear them. There is one extra phrase.

They're kind of cool.	
They're not exactly my colour.	
... but they seem a bit too bright.	
They're not really me.	
They're all right.	1
They're sort of ... different.	
They're quite nice.	
I actually prefer darker colours.	

c Work with a partner.
Student A: Turn to page 120.
Student B: Turn to page 123.

Portfolio 9 Writing about your opinions

a Read Natalia's email to a newspaper. How does Natalia feel about photo manipulation?

To: letters@editionmagazine.org
Subject: photo manipulation

Dear Editor

Yesterday I read an article about photo manipulation in beauty advertisements and I am writing to you because **I feel shocked by** some of the things mentioned.

Firstly, **it seems to me that** photo manipulation has a very negative effect on the way we see ourselves. The models in the magazines look perfect and we feel as if we have got to be just like them. Real people do not really look like the models in the photos because most of the images have been changed with photo-editing software.

In addition to this, **I am very surprised at** the high number of young people who want cosmetic surgery. I do not think that we should worry so much about changing our appearance. If magazines included more photos of celebrities looking normal, then **I am sure** that we would feel happier about the way we look.

In conclusion, magazine and advertising companies should think about the effect that their photos have on young people. **In my view**, they should use images that have not been altered, to help young people feel good about their own bodies and faces and try to get across the message that even supermodels are not perfect.

Natalia Allen, 17.

b Read the email again and complete the table with the expressions in **bold**.

Ordering ideas	Expressing your opinion
• First of all	• I (do not) think
•	• I (do not) believe
• Secondly	• ....
•	• ....
• To sum up	• ....
•	• ....
	• ....

c There are four paragraphs in the email. Which paragraph ...

introduces ideas? ☐

ends the email? ☐

adds more ideas? ☐

explains the reason for writing? ☐

d Write to a newspaper about one of the topics in the box. Use the expressions in Exercise b and the structure in Exercise c.

photos in adverts for clothes and shoes
graffiti
photos in fashion magazines
advertising on websites

e Work with a partner. Read what your partner has written. Do you agree with his/her opinions? Why? / Why not?

CRASH 🔊 3.11

QUICK! FOLLOW ME! WE CAN GO THIS WAY!

HEY! I THINK I CAN HEAR WATER!

THIS WAY. IT'S A RIVER.

MAYBE THE GHOSTS WANT TO HELP US ...

THEY WALKED ALL NIGHT.

WE'VE BEEN WALKING FOR HOURS!

STOP COMPLAINING, BEN!

I CAN SMELL SOMETHING ... IT SMELLS LIKE ... SMOKE.

SOMEONE MUST LIVE NEAR HERE. COME ON!

FINALLY ...

COME ON, BEN!

JUST A MINUTE! I WANT TO TAKE A PHOTO.

ARTHUR STOPPED IN SHOCK.

WHAT? IT CAN'T BE THEM!

OUR HELICOPTER'S JUST SPOTTED THE PLANE IN THE FOREST. THE RESCUERS ARE ON THEIR WAY TO IT NOW.

WE'LL BE THERE IN HALF AN HOUR.

IT LOOKS LIKE YOUR FRIEND'S GOING TO BE OK. YOU'RE ALL REALLY LUCKY TO BE ALIVE. OTHER KIDS HAVE DIED IN THAT FOREST.

WHAT DO YOU MEAN?

Reported statements
Reported questions, commands and requests
Vocabulary: Reading materials; Adverbs and adverbial phrases
Interaction 10: Checking details

1 Read and listen

a Read the texts quickly. How many versions of Shakespeare's plays are mentioned? Which would you like to see? Why?

1

RAPPING SHAKESPEARE

Plays from the sixteenth century are boring, right? Wrong, says rapper Akala, who has loved both Shakespeare and hip hop since he was at school. He thinks both use powerful rhythms to get across messages about timeless themes like love, money, jealousy, friendship, passion and revenge.

Akala believes that many teenagers are turned off Shakespeare because they only read his words on the page in school. Hip Hop Shakespeare is his project to bring the beat to the bard. He organises rapping workshops where young people use Shakespeare's original plots, but rewrite the words so they sound like hip hop.

Come and see the results at the Hip Hop Shakespeare event at London's South Bank Centre on 25th July. You can join in and rap along with Akala and his big sister, hip hop star Ms Dynamite!

2

Romeo and Juliet Act 2, Scene 2

ORIGINAL TEXT

Juliet

'Tis but thy name that is my enemy.
Thou art thyself, though not a Montague.
What's Montague? It is nor hand, nor foot,
Nor arm, nor face, nor any other part
Belonging to a man. O, be some other name!
What's in a name? That which we call a rose
By any other name would smell as sweet.
So Romeo would, were he not Romeo called,
Retain that dear perfection which he owes
Without that title. Romeo, doff thy name,
And for that name, which is no part of thee
Take all myself.

Romeo

I take thee at thy word.
Call me but love, and I'll be new baptised.
Henceforth I never will be Romeo.

3

Romeo and Juliet Act 2, Scene 2

MODERN VERSION

JULIET

It's only your name that is my enemy. You are yourself, whether or not you are a Montague. What's a Montague anyway? It isn't a hand, a foot, an arm, a face, or any other part of a man. Oh, take another name!

What does a name matter? A rose would smell just as sweet if we called it something else. Romeo would be just as perfect if he wasn't called Romeo. Romeo, change your name. Your name really has nothing to do with you – get rid of your name and take me instead!

ROMEO

I believe you're telling the truth. If you call me your love, I'll change my name. From now on, I'll never be called Romeo again.

b 🔊 **3.12** Read the texts again and listen. Are the sentences *right* (✓), *wrong* (✗) or *doesn't say* (–)?

1 Akala thinks the subject-matter of Shakepeare's plays is outdated.
2 The Hip Hop Shakespeare project changes the words in the plays.
3 Writing plays made Shakespeare world-famous and rich.
4 Romeo's family name is Montague.
5 Juliet thinks the names of things are very important.
6 Romeo wants Juliet to love him.

c Find the words and phrases in the texts that mean …

1 never becoming old or outdated (text 1)
2 another word for the story in a book, play or film (text 1)
3 remove or throw away something unwanted (text 3)
4 from this moment and always in the future (text 3)

d Work with a partner. Answer the questions.

1 Have you ever seen a Shakespeare play in the theatre or in the cinema, as a film? Which play was it? What was it about? Did you like it? Why? / Why not?
2 What type of live performances do you like going to see?

② Pronunciation (D·V·D)

Rhythm

a 🔊 **3.13** Listen to part of a hip hop version of *Romeo and Juliet*.

Sweet <u>Juliet</u> your <u>face</u> is <u>like</u> a <u>rose</u>.
But <u>do</u> you <u>love</u> me? <u>Tell</u> me, <u>no</u> one <u>knows</u>.

b 🔊 **3.13** Listen again and repeat. Stress the <u>underlined</u> syllables.

c 🔊 **3.14** Listen to the next part and <u>underline</u> the stressed syllables.

Oh Romeo my heart won't be the same.
Hey let's get married, boy! I'll change my name.

d 🔊 **3.15** Listen to both parts and repeat.

③ Vocabulary

Reading materials

a 🔊 **3.16** Match the words with the definitions. Then listen and check.

1 autobiography	2 biography	3 e-book
4 graphic novel	5 non-fiction	6 novel
7 screenplay	8 thriller	

A a book about the life of a real person
B a piece of writing for the cinema
C a book about imaginary people and events
D writing that is about real events and facts
E a book about the writer's own life
F an electronic book
G a book with an exciting story, often about crime
H a book which tells a story in pictures

b Do you know any other words for reading materials? Write them down.

c What kind of reading materials would you recommend for someone who …

1 likes reading about the lives of famous people?
2 wants to work in the film industry?
3 loves action and mystery stories?
4 prefers looking at pictures to reading texts?
5 likes using the latest technology?

Culture Vulture

Did you know that 83% of 11–18 year-olds in Britain read in their free time? However, 70% would prefer to watch TV or a DVD than read a book. Do you read in your free time? Would you prefer to watch a DVD or read a book?

(4) Grammar Reported statements

a Look at the examples of direct speech and reported statements and complete the table with the correct verb forms and adverbial phrases.

> ⤑ *'It's only your name that is my enemy.'*
>   → *Juliet said it was only his name that was her enemy.*
>
> *'I'll change my name.'*
>   → *Romeo said he would change his name.*
>
> *'I can come here tomorrow.'*
>   → *He said he could come there the next day.*

Direct speech		Reported statements
Present simple	→	....
Present continuous	→	Past continuous
Present perfect	→	Past perfect
Past simple	→	Past perfect
will	→	....
can	→	....
tomorrow	→	....
yesterday	→	*the day before*
here	→	....
this morning	→	*that morning*
next Monday	→	*the following Monday*

Grammar reference: Workbook page 98

b Report these statements.

1 'I've been here before.'
  She said ....

2 'I'm going to Verona next Sunday.'
  He told me ....

3 'We're exhausted.'
  They said ....

4 'I'll do it tomorrow.'
  I said ....

5 'I went to the new sushi restaurant yesterday.'
  He told me ....

6 'We don't buy a newspaper every day.'
  You said ....

Check it out!

- We need an object after *tell*.
  She **told him** that she loved him.
  NOT ~~She told that she loved him~~.
- We don't include an object after *say*.
  She **said** that she loved him.
  NOT ~~She said him that she loved him~~.

(5) Speak

a Number the activities from what you do most (1) to what you do least (4).

reading books ☐   reading newspapers ☐
reading magazines or comics ☐
writing text messages ☐

b Work with a partner. Compare your order for Exercise 5a and ask follow-up questions.

How long do you spend … a week? How often do you … ? What type of … do you like? Why?

c Work with a partner. Ask and answer the questions and ask follow-up questions.

1 What was the last thing you read?
2 What was the last thing you watched on TV?

> ⤑ A: *What was the last thing you read?*
>   B: *A magazine article about personality types.*
>   A: *Was it interesting?*

d Work with a different partner. Tell your new partner what your first partner said. Use reported speech.

> ⤑ *He told me he'd read a magazine article about personality types. He said it …*

6 Vocabulary Adverbs and adverbial phrases

a Read a summary of a manga story. What type of story is it? Would you like to read it? Why? / Why not?

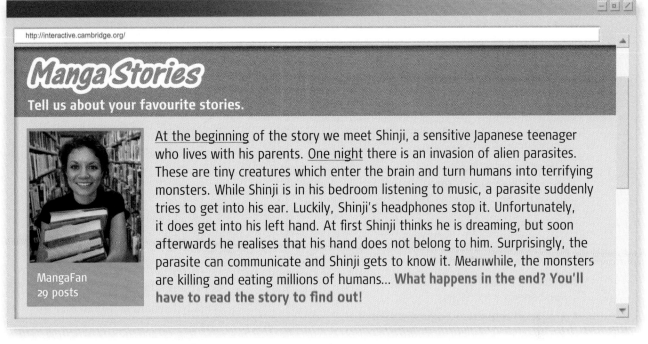

http://interactive.cambridge.org/

Manga Stories
Tell us about your favourite stories.

At the beginning of the story we meet Shinji, a sensitive Japanese teenager who lives with his parents. **One night** there is an invasion of alien parasites. These are tiny creatures which enter the brain and turn humans into terrifying monsters. While Shinji is in his bedroom listening to music, a parasite suddenly tries to get into his ear. Luckily, Shinji's headphones stop it. Unfortunately, it does get into his left hand. At first Shinji thinks he is dreaming, but soon afterwards he realises that his hand does not belong to him. Surprisingly, the parasite can communicate and Shinji gets to know it. Meanwhile, the monsters are killing and eating millions of humans... **What happens in the end? You'll have to read the story to find out!**

MangaFan
29 posts

b Find and <u>underline</u> nine more adverbs and adverbial phrases in the text.

c 🔊 **3.17** Add the expressions from Exercise 6b under the correct heading. Then listen and check.

Showing when or how things happened	Expressing opinions
at the beginning one night	luckily

d Circle the correct words.

1 My best friend and I fell out last year, but *at first / in the end* we made up again.

2 *Luckily / Unfortunately*, their latest album is a big disappointment.

3 *Suddenly / Meanwhile* a dog ran in front of the car and I had no time to react, so I hit it.

4 *While / Meanwhile* the guards were sleeping, we managed to escape.

5 She published her first novel last year and *soon afterwards / luckily* she bought her new car.

6 He was sitting at home reading a thriller, unaware of the real danger. *While / Meanwhile*, the aliens were gradually getting nearer and nearer.

e Work with a partner. Think of something you've read or watched recently. Tell your partner what happened, using adverbs and adverbial phrases.

7 Listen

a 🔊 **3.18** Listen to the interviews with teenagers for a radio programme and circle the reading materials they talk about.

(online) magazines   manga
(online) newspapers   novels   poems
non-fiction   song lyrics   plays   blogs

b 🔊 **3.18** Listen again and answer the questions.

1 What day is *World Book Day*?
2 What does Jessica prefer reading?
3 What do Jessica and Vicky like reading online?
4 What type of book does Drew say is popular in the USA?
5 What does Tom read online?
6 Why does he like the bookshop?
7 What is Ruby's ideal way of spending Saturday morning?

c Work in a group. Discuss the questions.

1 Do teenagers in your country read the same types of thing as the teenagers in the radio programme?
2 How often do you go to bookshops or libraries? Where else do you find interesting things to read?

8 Grammar

Reported questions, commands and requests

a Look at the examples. Then (circle) the correct words to complete the rules.

⟶ *'**Do** you **like** reading?'*
→ Ruby **asked him if/whether** he **liked** reading.
*'**What do** you **like** reading?'*
→ She **asked her what** she **liked** reading.
*'**Can you recommend** some manga?'*
→ She **asked him to recommend** some manga.
*'**Speak up** a little.'*
→ Ruby **told him to speak up** a little.

- In reported questions, we use **question / statement** word order.
- When we report *yes/no* questions we **use / don't use** *if* or *whether*.
- We report **requests / commands** with *ask* someone *to* + infinitive.
- We report **requests / commands** with *tell* someone *to* + infinitive.

Grammar reference: Workbook page 98

Check it out!

We sometimes have to change pronouns when we report questions, requests and commands.
'Do **you** want to come with **us**?' →
He asked me if **I** wanted to go with **them**.

b Rewrite the sentences as reported questions or commands. Use *ask* or *tell*.

1 'Excuse me, where's King Street?'
   The man asked her _____

2 'Give me your essays, please.'
   Mr Jones told us _____

3 'Why can't you come to our party?'
   Jess asked us _____

4 'Go away!'
   She _____

5 'Do you like hip hop?'
   Mike _____

c Work with a partner. Ask and answer questions and ask follow-up questions.

What type of books do you like?
Do you like texting?
How often do you use social networking sites?
Do you write a blog or a diary?

d Work with a different partner. Report what you asked your partner in Exercise 8c and his/her answers.

⟶ *I asked him if he liked texting. He told me that he did.*

Interaction 10 (DVD) Checking details

a 🔊 3.19 Listen to the conversation between Mel, Leah and Ethan. What are they talking about?

a theatre school   seeing a play   a theatre festival

b 🔊 3.19 Listen again and tick (✓) the phrases you hear.

1 Introducing a topic	2 Checking
You know that …	What do we have to do?
I wanted to ask you …	
I'm calling to check …	Did you say £30?

3 Asking someone to repeat something
What did you say?
Sorry, I didn't get that.
Can you say that again?

c Work with a partner.
Student A: Turn to page 120.
Student B: Turn to page 123.

Portfolio 10

A book review

a Read the review of *Dracula*. Would you like to read it?
If you have already read it, do you agree with the review?

Book reviewer   ▬ □ ✕

Dracula, published in 1897, was the first vampire bestseller. It is the most famous novel by Bram Stoker, who researched ancient legends about Dracula before he wrote his terrifying story.

At the beginning of the story, a young Englishman, Jonathan Harker, travels on business to Count Dracula's castle in Transylvania, Romania. At first Jonathan finds the Count polite and friendly, but soon afterwards he discovers that not everything is what it appears to be. Why are there no mirrors? Why isn'tvDracula's prisoner. One night, while he is trying to get out of the castle, three beautiful female vampires attack him.

Meanwhile, Dracula is in England and is following Jonathan's girlfriend, Mina, and her friend Lucy. When Lucy becomes mysteriously ill, her doctor sends for his old teacher, Professor Van Helsing. Luckily, Van Helsing is an expert on vampires and he finds two small marks on Lucy's neck. After a strange attack by a wolf, Lucy seems to die, but Van Helsing knows that she isn't dead. She has become a vampire.

Read the novel to find out what happens next. Although the middle of the book is a little slow, the end is exciting. The story is told from the point of view of different characters, which makes it more original. Bram Stoker also uses different text types, like letters, diaries and newspaper articles. If you like vampire stories, you should definitely read this classic.

---

b Complete the table. Tick (✓) the first column if the book review includes the information. Write the paragraph number in the second column if appropriate.

	Tick (✓) if included	Paragraph(s)
Information about the author		
Information about the main character(s)		
Details about the beginning of the story		
Details about the end of the story		
Why the book is good / bad		
A recommendation		

c Which things in the table are **not** included? Why not?

d Write a review of a book you have read.
- Include the information given in Exercise b.
- Use adverbs and adverbial phrases.
- Use reported speech if necessary.

e Read your partner's book review. Would you like to read the book?

1

Edinburgh International Festival

Each summer people visit Edinburgh from all over the world and enjoy three exciting weeks of the very best in international opera, music, drama and dance.

Come with us on a journey of discovery and celebrate the colour, the passion and the drama of the Edinburgh International Festival.

See performers from the Americas and the Pacific as well as artists from Spain, Holland, Germany, Russia and the UK.

We'd love you to join us!

2

Shakespeare for Breakfast

Tickets from **£5.50**

VENUE: C
FESTIVAL: EDINBURGH FESTIVAL FRINGE
CATEGORY: THEATRE

Running time: 0:55

The Bardic Breakfasters are back! C's Shakespearean sensation returns for an 18th sell-out year with free coffee and croissants!

'Bouncy and boisterous take on Willie's work' *List*.
'Well worth getting out of bed for' *Independent*.

3

About the Royal Edinburgh Military Tattoo

4

EDINBURGH INTERNATIONAL BOOK FESTIVAL

An inspiring literary festival, the world's largest public celebration of the written word, right in the heart of Edinburgh: hundreds of author events, debates and workshops packed into 17 extraordinary days each August.

ROBERT LOUIS STEVENSON'S STRANGE CASE OF Dr Jekyll and Mr Hyde

adapted by Alan Grant
illustrated by Cam Kennedy

Missed an event at the Book Festival?

You needn't miss out as you can now download the audio to some of our most popular events from our media archive. If you don't have time to listen to a whole event, why not catch the flavour of the festival with podcast interviews or read about memorable moments on our blog. You can also visit our image gallery:
http://www.edbookfest.co.uk/

Against the world-famous backdrop of Edinburgh Castle the Royal Military Tattoo will celebrate their Diamond Jubilee this year. The landmark 60th anniversary production will feature awe-inspiring colour and variety from the four corners of the globe.

Edinburgh Military Tattoo fact file:

More than 12 million people have attended the Tattoo in the last 60 years. The annual audience is around 217,000.

Around 100 million people see the Tattoo each year on international television.

Approximately 70 per cent of each audience is from outside Scotland. Half of these are from overseas.

The Tattoo has always been staged at Edinburgh Castle.

Rehearsals take place at Redford Barracks in Edinburgh.

Over 40 countries have been represented at the Tattoo.

5

Mercat Tours of Edinburgh

*W*e provide the best Ghost and History tours in Scotland and specialise in walking tours around Edinburgh's Old Town featuring the most haunted locations, the scariest stories and most spectacular candlelit Underground Vaults.

Our tours run all year round. When you visit Edinburgh join us for a journey back in time to experience the dark past of Scotland's capital city.

Ticket type	Price (each)
Adult	£9.00
Concession	£7.50
Child	£5.00
Family	£23.00
Adult Extended Tour	£11.00
Child Extended Tour	£6.50
Family Extended Tour	£28.50

6

Edinburgh Book Swap

To mark the 500 years of printing and publishing in Scotland, Publishing Scotland – the industry and promotion body for publishers in Scotland – teamed up with Edinburgh University and the Edinburgh UNESCO City of Literature team to run a massive **Book Swap** in the City on **Tuesday 1 April**.

Edinburgh residents, visitors and workers **took along a book** they would like to recommend or swap and picked up another to take home. The **event was free** and Scottish publishers donated over 500 books of all kinds to get things started – children's books, books on Scottish history, walking guides, biography, academic, sport, novels . . . something for everyone.

1 Culture UK: Edinburgh

a Look at the information about Edinburgh and answer the questions.

1 What is the name of the musical military parade? Where does it take place?
2 What do you get for breakfast at the Shakespeare show?
3 What four nationalities, apart from the UK, are definitely taking part at the Edinburgh International Festival this year?
4 How long does the Book Festival last?
5 How long have books been published in Edinburgh? How is the anniversary being celebrated?
6 If you miss an event at the Book Festival, what can you do?
7 Which part of Edinburgh does the Mercat Tour visit? What is the highlight of the tour?

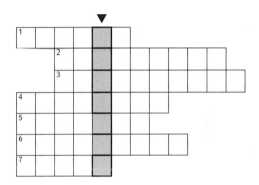
Edinburgh

b Complete the crossword and find the name of the symbol of Scotland.

1 give something to a charity (text 6)
2 a practice before a show (text 3)
3 with a lot of energy (text 3)
4 foreign, from abroad (text 3)
5 with ghosts (text 5)
6 lit by candles (text 5)
7 the earth or the world (text 3)

c Work with a partner. Would you like to visit Edinburgh? Which events would you like to go to?

2 Your project

An arts festival

a Work in a group. Plan a festival like the Edinburgh International Festival for your town/area. Think about:

- the type of festival. It could be one type or several different types.

  book   music   theatre   comedy   film   (other)

- any extra attractions, e.g. special tours
- the location
- the name of the festival
- where people can stay
- how to get there and how to get around

b Make a poster about your festival. Include the information from Exercise 2a and pictures or photos if possible.

Review ⑨ and ⑩

① Grammar

a Complete the sentences with one word: *like*, *as* or *though*.

1 What a great camera! Those look .... professional photos.

2 This street is familiar. I feel .... if I've been here before.

3 What's all that noise? It sounds as .... they're having an argument.

4 This T-shirt feels .... silk, but it's cotton.

5 We should listen to your brother. He sounds .... though he knows a lot about computers.

6 You've got a new mobile .... mine. When did you get it? ☐ 6

b Complete the text with *a*, *an*, *the* or no article.

¹........................... Dutch painter Van Gogh is ²........................... fascinating artist. At first, he only painted with ³........................... dark colours, until he saw some colourful paintings from ⁴........................... Japan. He was impressed by ⁵........................... paintings and started using ⁶........................... brighter colours in his own work. He moved to ⁷........................... south of France, where he painted his well-known paintings of ⁸........................... sunflowers. Unfortunately, he became very unhappy and after an argument with a friend he cut of part of ⁹........................... ear. He died in ¹⁰........................... 1890. While he was alive, Van Gogh sold only one painting. However, since his death he has become one of ¹¹........................... most famous artists in ¹²........................... world. ☐ 6

c What did they say? Rewrite the reported statements in direct speech.

1 They said they had been there before.
'We .... ,'

2 She said she was going to write a graphic novel.
'I .... ,'

3 He said he would teach me how to drive.
'I .... ,'

4 You said you couldn't play the piano.
'I .... ,'

5 They said they always went to that cinema.
'We .... ,'

6 He said he was going to see his cousin the next day.
'I .... ,' ☐ 6

d Write the underlined questions and commands as reported questions or commands.

James: ¹ What do we have to do for homework?

Alice: We have to write about a book. ² What's your favourite book? ³ What type of books do you like?

James: I don't really read books.

Alice: OK. ⁴ Write about the book we read in class. ⁵ Have you finished it?

James: Well … not exactly.

Alice: ⁶ Finish the book, then you can write about it.

1 James asked Alice ....

2 Alice asked James ....

3 She asked him ....

4 She told him ....

5 She asked him ....

6 She told him .... ☐ 6

e Read the text about Livi. Choose the correct answer: A, B, C or D.

Livi is ¹........... fascinating teenage writer and artist. I feel ²........... I know her through her poems and her art. When I interviewed her online she ³........... me that she had been drawing since she ⁴........... hold a crayon. She said that sometimes she feels as ⁵........... she is as light as air and art is the magic that lifts her feet from the ground. She also told me that she ⁶........... reading short stories.

1	A an	B a	C the	D (–)
2	A if	B though	C as though	D as
3	A told	B telling	C says	D said
4	A can	B is able to	C will	D could
5	A like	B if	C as though	D well
6	A love	B is loving	C was loving	D loved

☐ 6

How are you doing?

How many points have you got? Put two crosses on the chart: one for grammar and one for vocabulary.

2 Vocabulary

a Match the adjectives with the descriptions.

> amusing   annoying   confusing   depressing
> fascinating   gorgeous   impressive   shocking

1 It's so difficult to understand! ....
2 It's very interesting. ....
3 It makes me really sad. ....
4 It makes me laugh. ....
5 He makes me angry. ....
6 She's really beautiful. ....
7 It's surprising and upsetting. ....
8 It really impresses me. ....

☐ 8

b Complete the puzzle and use the ◯ letters to find the mystery word.

1 You can trust her. She tells the ....
2 That painting isn't a Picasso – it's ....
3 He told her a .... and said he liked her haircut because he didn't want to upset her.
4 It's against the law to .... someone's signature.
5 That film uses really clever camera .... You feel like you're flying through the air.
6 Don't let the adverts .... you!
7 Mystery word – someone who never tells lies is ....

1 ☐☐◯☐◯
2 ◯☐☐☐
3 ☐☐☐◯☐   ☐☐☐
4 ☐☐◯☐☐
5 ◯☐☐☐☐☐
6 ☐☐☐◯☐

(text 6)

7 ☐☐☐☐☐☐u☐☐   ☐ 7

GREEN: Great! Tell your teacher your score!
YELLOW: Not bad, but go to the website for extra practice.
RED: Talk to your teacher and look at Units 9 and 10 again. Go to the website for extra practice.

| 14 | 15 | 16 | 17 | 18 | 19 | 20 | 21 | 22 | 23 | 24 | 25 | 26 | 27 | 28 | 29 | 30 |

| 14 | 15 | 16 | 17 | 18 | 19 | 20 | 21 | 22 | 23 | 24 | 25 | 26 | 27 | 28 | 29 | 30 |

---

c Add vowels (*a, e, i, o, u*) to make words for reading material.

1 thr_ll_r
2 b_ _gr_phy
3 _ -b_ _k
4 gr_ph_c n_v_l
5 _ _t_b_ _gr_phy
6 n_n-f_ct_ _n
7 scr_ _npl_y
8 n_v_l
9 pl_ y   ☐ 9

d ⟲Circle the correct words.

The manga *Aventura 1* tells the story of Lewin, a student at the Gaius school for witches and wizards. [1] *Unfortunately / Luckily* Lewin has no magical talent, but [2] *surprisingly / unfortunately* he is accepted into the top school of magic. [3] *Meanwhile / At first* he finds it difficult, but he doesn't give up. [4] *Soon afterwards / In the end* he makes friends with Soela and Chris and [5] *suddenly / luckily* they teach him the methods of magic. [6] *At first / In the end* they realise that Lewin has hidden talents and could become a great wizard.   ☐ 6

Correct it!

Correct these typical learner errors from Units 9 and 10.

1 They will live like if they were in prison.

....

2 It seemed as they knew each other.

....

3 I've enjoyed a trip very much.

....

4 He is studying economics at the Oxford University.

....

5 Simon suddenly realised how lucky he was.

....

6 My cousin said us to wait.

....

7 He told that the story was true.

....

8 You asked me wether I had bought a computer or a bicycle.

....

9 It was really impressing to see the midnight sun.

....

10 Please tell me the true.

....

11 Is it a crime?

Subject and object questions
wish and *if only*
Vocabulary: Crime; Crime collocations
Interaction 11: Apologising

1 Vocabulary Crime

a 🔊 **3.20** Match the crimes with the definitions. Then listen and check.

1 bank robbery	2 burglary	3 hacking
4 identity theft	5 piracy	6 plagiarism
7 shoplifting	8 theft	9 vandalism

A taking or stealing something

B getting into someone else's computer system

C stealing money from a bank

D copying software, music or films from the internet without permission

E stealing things from a shop

F breaking things or writing graffiti in public places

G getting into a building and stealing things

H copying someone else's work or idea

I stealing personal information about someone else and using it to commit a crime

b 🔊 **3.21** Write down the criminals and verbs for the crimes in Exercise 1a. Use a dictionary to help if necessary. Then listen and check.

c Change the word in brackets to a verb or noun to fit into the sentence.

1 A .... (burgle) stole our computer.

2 The bank .... (rob) was caught.

3 Why do people .... (vandal) buses?

4 A .... (theft) stole my purse.

5 Don't .... (plagiarist) someone else's work in your essay.

6 A .... (hack) got into the bank's computer.

7 The police arrested her for .... (shoplift).

8 It's quite easy to .... (piracy) DVDs.

> ### Check it out!
>
> • You *rob* a person or a place. You *steal* a thing.
>   They **robbed** the bank.
>   NOT ~~They stole the bank~~.
>   They **stole** the money.
>   NOT ~~They robbed the money~~.

2 Listen

a Work with a partner. Do the quiz.

CRIME QUIZ

1 **Who wears green T-shirts that say *I'm a thief* in Ohio, USA?**
  A burglars   B bank robbers   C shoplifters

2 **Where do you need a licence to skateboard?**
  A London   B Florida   C Hong Kong

3 **Who has to pay a fine in Russia? People with ...**
  A broken mobiles   B dirty cars   C more than two computers

4 **Where is it legal to escape from prison?**
  A The USA   B France   C Denmark

5 **What was illegal in Singapore before 2004?**
  A chewing gum   B smoking   C burgers

6 **What do some students study at one university in Britain?**
  A hacking   B burglary   C vandalism

b 🔊 **3.22** Listen to the TV quiz show and check your answers.

c 🔊 **3.22** Listen again and answer the questions.

1 What's the maximum number of points for each question in the quiz?

2 Who gives the wrong answer to question four?

3 Why was it illegal to chew gum in one place?

4 Where in Britain can students do a university degree in hacking?

5 Which team wins the quiz?

6 How many points do they get?

d Work with a partner. Answer the questions.

1 Would you like to go on a TV quiz show? Why? / Why not?

2 Which laws in the quiz do you think are the weirdest? Why?

3 Grammar

Subject and object questions

a Look at the examples. Then (circle) the correct words to complete the rules.

Subject questions	Object questions
1 *Who **wears** green T-shirts in Ohio?*	1 *What **do** shoplifters **wear** in Ohio?*
2 *Which team **won** the quiz?*	2 *How many points **did** Team A **get**?*
3 *Who **has to pay** a fine in Russia?*	3 *What **do** people with dirty cars **have to do** in Russia?*

- In subject questions, the question word is the **subject / object** of the verb.
- We use a question word + verb in **subject / object** questions.
- We always use an auxiliary verb (e.g. *do, did, had*) in **subject / object** questions.

Grammar reference: Workbook page 100

Check it out!

- In subject questions with *Who* and *What*, the verb is usually singular even if the answer is plural.
  Who **wants** a drink? We all want a drink.
  NOT ~~Who want a drink?~~
  What's in the fridge? Some cheese and some apples.
  NOT ~~What are in the fridge?~~

b Add an auxiliary verb in the gaps where necessary. Then match the questions with the answers.

twenty   Ben   hacking   skateboarders   Ben   Team A won

1 Who .... needs a licence in Florida?
2 What .... some students study at university in Scotland?
3 Who .... gave the wrong answer in the quiz?
4 What .... happened at the end of the quiz?
5 How many points .... Team B get?
6 Who .... Rosie tell off?

c Make subject or object questions from the prompts.

1 Who / you / chat to / at school?
   <u>Who do you chat to at school?</u>

2 What / make / you / happy?
   <u>What makes you happy?</u>

3 Who / help / you / with your homework?
4 Who / oversleep / in your family?
5 Which films / you / find / amusing?
6 Who / send / you / text messages?
7 What / plagiarism / mean?
8 When / you / last / go to the cinema?

d Work with a partner. Answer the questions in Exercise 3c.

4 Pronunciation DVD

Consonant clusters at the ends of words

a 🔊 3.23 Listen to the words and repeat.

vandali**sm**	the**ft**	hac**ks**	bur**gles**
/zm/	/ft/	/ks/	/glz/

b 🔊 3.24 Listen and (circle) the words you hear. Then listen, check and repeat.

A	B
1 shoplift	shoplifts
2 arrest	arrests
3 uncle	uncles
4 accept	accepts
5 send	sends
6 argument	arguments
7 act	acts
8 ask	asks

c Work with a partner. Student A: say one of the words in Exercise 4b. Student B: give the reference for the word. Then change roles.

uncle   A-3

d 🔊 3.25 Listen and repeat.

The artist objects to his arrests for vandalism and plagiarism, but accepts his arrest for theft.

(5) Vocabulary
Crime collocations

a 🔊 **3.26** Complete the crime collocations with the words in the box. Then listen and check.

> a fine   a suspect   charge   community   crime   law   prison   record   sentence   youth

1 If you do something illegal, you **commit a** _____ or **break the** _____ .

2 The police **arrest** _____ and take him/her to a police station when they think he/she is responsible for a crime.

3 The police _____ **someone with a crime** when they officially say that he/she has done something illegal.

4 When criminals **go to** _____ or **jail** they live in a building with other criminals and they cannot leave.

5 A special prison for young criminals is called a _____ **prison**.

6 A **prison** _____ is the length of time a criminal spends in prison.

7 A typical punishment for a crime that is not very serious is to **pay** _____ .

8 A common punishment for young criminals is to help people in their area by doing _____ **service**.

9 An official document listing the crimes someone has committed is a **criminal** _____ .

Check it out!

- For words that end in a vowel + consonant, double the consonant before -ed, -ing, -er, -est.
  commit – commi**tt**ed
  shop – sho**pp**ing   rob – ro**bb**er
  regret – regre**tt**ed   big – bi**gg**est

b Complete the story with the correct form of the words.

> arrest   charge   commit   crime   criminal   law   prison   sentence

Last summer three youths [1]_____ a serious [2]_____ . They broke into a house and stole a computer, a TV, a microwave and over one hundred DVDs. The police [3]_____ the suspects, took them to the police station and [4]_____ them with burglary. The youths were found guilty and were given a long prison [5]_____ . As well as going to [6]_____ , they will have a [7]_____ record for the rest of their lives for breaking the [8]_____ .

c Work with a partner. Answer the questions.

1 What happens to people under 18 in your country who commit a serious crime?

2 Do you think community service is a good type of punishment? Why? / Why not?

(6) Speak

a Work with a partner. Look at the crimes and the punishments. What do you think the punishment should be for young people under 18 for each crime?

Crimes
- drive a car without a licence
- steal a magazine from a shop
- not buy a ticket for the bus or train
- plagiarise an essay for school from the internet
- vandalise a shop window with spray paint

Punishments
- pay a fine
- do community service
- get detention at school
- get suspended from school
- get told off by the police
- get arrested by the police
- go to a youth prison

b Work in a group. Compare your ideas with the rest of your group and explain your reasons. Then agree together on a punishment for each crime.

⋯⟩ A: *I think that students who plagiarise essays should get suspended from school.*
  B: *I completely disagree. I think they should fail the essay and get detention at school.*
  C: *I see what you mean, but I think ...*

c Tell the class your group's decisions. Agree on a punishment for each crime with the whole class.

(7) Read and listen

a Read the text quickly and (circle) the crimes and punishments in the text.

News	World	Politics
	Technology	Sport

Computer criminals

As more and more of us depend on the internet for everything from shopping to keeping in touch with friends and family, more and more of our personal information is stored online. This means that we are all possible targets for hackers, and hacking laws are becoming stricter to protect us. Consequently, in the future more young hackers could find themselves going to prison for their crimes. In 2005, a teenage hacker from Massachusetts was sentenced to 11 months in a youth jail for hacking into Paris Hilton's mobile phone and putting a copy of her address book online, which included email addresses of celebrity friends like Eminem and Christina Aguilera. As well as having a criminal record for the rest of his life, the 17-year-old was banned from using a computer or mobile phone for two years.

In 2008, 18-year-olds Omar Khan and Tanvir Singh were charged with breaking into their high school and hacking into the computer network. Khan used stolen IDs and passwords to cheat on tests and to change his average C and D grades into A grades. He wanted to make sure he got into university, but teachers became suspicious when they noticed he suddenly had some of the best marks in the school. He spent graduation day in prison instead of celebrating with his classmates.

A group of about ten students were involved in the cheating and grade changing, but unlike the others, who were all under 18, Khan and Singh were charged with their crimes as adults. Singh only broke into the school once. He completed 200 hours of community service and three years of probation, and all charges against him were eventually dropped. But Khan faced a sentence of prison time, probation, community service and fines.

Michael Calce, who was also a teen hacker, now wishes he hadn't committed his crimes. At just 15, he hacked into some of the biggest sites on the internet, including Yahoo!, Amazon, CNN and eBay. He didn't steal money or information, but he shut down the sites to show the world that computer security was vulnerable to attack. He was arrested in 2000 and later regretted what he had done. He now wishes people would take hacking more seriously. He has written books that teach ways we can protect ourselves against hacking.

b 3.27 Read the text again and listen. Then answer the questions.

1 What do the numbers and letters refer to in the text?

> 11   18   C   A   15

2 Why are hacking laws changing?
3 What happened to Paris Hilton?
4 Why did Khan want to hack into the school computer network?
5 How did the teachers find out about the hacking?
6 Why did one ex-hacker write a book?

c Find the words in the text that mean ...

1 people who other people attack (para 1)
2 another word for school marks (para 2)
3 thinking that someone might have done something wrong or dishonest (para 2)
4 a period of time when a criminal must behave well in order to avoid being sent to prison (para 3)
5 felt sorry about something you did (para 4)

d Work in a group. Answer the questions.

1 Do you think teenage criminals should go to prison? Why? / Why not?
2 Do you think that hacking laws need to be stricter nowadays? Why? / Why not?

8 Grammar *wish* and *if only*

a Look at the examples. Then (circle) the correct words to complete the rules.

> ⟶ *I wish I had better grades.*
> *He wishes he hadn't committed his crimes.*
> *He wishes people would take hacking more seriously.*
> *If only he hadn't committed his crimes!*

We use *wish/if only*:
- + past simple for a **present** / **past** situation which we would like to be different but can't change.
- + *would* for something we would like to happen in the present or **past** / **future**.
- + past perfect for a situation in the **present** / **past** that we regret but **can** / **can't** change.

Grammar reference: Workbook page 88

Check it out!

- *If only* is similar to *wish* but stronger.
  I wish I could go on holiday. = I would like to.
  If only I could go on holiday! = I would really like to!

b Complete Lisa's email with the correct form of the verbs.

```
To:       shona@zapmail.com
Subject:  stuff
```

Hi Shona

I'm feeling so depressed! I wish you ¹ .... (be) here with me now. If only your mum ² .... (let) you come round to my house now! I went to Angela's party last night. If only you ³ .... (come) with me. It was awful! That new girl Celia was there. I told her that I liked Jake and then she went up to Jake and told him! It was so embarrassing, I wish I ⁴ .... (not tell) her. He was with his friends and they all started laughing. I wish Celia ⁵ .... (not go) to the party. I'm never going to speak to her again!

Lisa ☹

c Look at the things Paolo isn't happy about. Complete the sentences with *wish/if only*.

1 Paolo doesn't have a computer in his room.
   He wishes ....
2 His e-pals can't speak Italian.
   If only ....
3 He has flu so can't go to the party.
   He wishes ....
4 His parents won't let him go out tonight.
   If only ....

d Complete the sentences so that they are true for you.

1 I wish I was … .
2 I wish I could … .
3 If only my parents wouldn't … .
4 If only I hadn't … .

Interaction 11 [DVD]

Apologising

a ◀)) 3.28 Listen to the conversation between Lara and her teacher. What is Lara apologising for? Why did she do it? What does her teacher decide should happen?

b ◀)) 3.28 Listen again and complete the phrases with the words in the box.

again	have	doesn't	good	really
want	was	wrong	your	

1 I .... to apologise for what I did.
2 You know that it's .... to copy.
3 I shouldn't .... copied.
4 I'm .... sorry.
5 I accept .... apology.
6 As long as it .... happen again.
7 I realise it .... wrong.
8 It won't happen ....
9 That's ....

c Work with a partner.
Student A: Turn to page 120.
Student B: Turn to page 123.

Portfolio 11　A report

a Read the report and choose the best heading for each paragraph.

1 What is this report about? / Who breaks the law?
2 Which artists give concerts online? / Where can people find music online?
3 How do people swap music? / Who commits crimes online?
4 What does the law say? / Which sites are legal?

Music online and the law

1 ....

The aim of this report is to **look at** where people can find music online, **explain** what they can do with music without breaking the law and **suggest** how they can protect their computer when accessing music sites online.

2 ....

There are many ways of accessing music online, from downloading tracks or albums to buying e-tickets. Some sites allow fans to listen to music to see if they like it before they buy it and some artists let people enjoy their music for free, but **most of the time**, music has to be paid for.

3 ....

Generally speaking, it is fine to swap music on P2P (peer-to-peer) networks if people follow copyright laws. However, one problem with these networks is that users are at risk of viruses or identity theft. Social networking pages can also be used to share videos, photos or music. Watching a video or listening to a song is **usually** fine, but downloading a track onto a computer could be against the law.

4 ....

To sum up, copyright laws protect artists, and artists depend on these laws to earn money for their work. **Because of this**, sharing copyrighted music without permission is against the law and the punishment is usually a huge fine. **For these reasons, I recommend that** people find out about copyright laws, make sure their computer is protected against viruses and only use legal sites online.

---

b Work with a partner. Answer the questions.

1 Is a report a formal or an informal piece of writing?
2 Who do you think would read a report?
3 How is the information organised in a report?

c Complete the table with the words and phrases in **bold** in the report.

Writing a report	
To begin the report and say what it does	• • • •
To give general information	• • •
To give reasons	• •
To give recommendations	•

Check it out!

● When you write a report, organise it into paragraphs.
  1 introduction to explain why you are writing the report
  2 your first piece of information
  3 a different piece of information
  4 your conclusion and recommendations

d Write a report about one of the topics in the box. Before you write, plan your ideas and organise them in four paragraphs.

> How to keep computer passwords safe
> Using the internet for homework and plagiarism
> Downloading films from the internet

e Work with a partner. Read your partner's report. Is it interesting? Are the ideas organised well?

Sensational Singapore

Key Facts

Official name Republic of Singapore

Capital City of Singapore

Location One main island and 63 tiny islands in Southeast Asia, between Malaysia and Indonesia.

Climate Tropical. Hot and sunny all year round, with two monsoon seasons.

Currency Singapore Dollar

Official language Malay, but English is the main language of communication. Other languages include Mandarin, Tamil and Singlish (Singaporean English!)

Internet country code .sg

The Merlion, Singapore's symbol: half-lion, half-fish

Singapore's skyline and Esplanade theatres.

---

1 ....

Unique is probably the best word to describe Singapore, as there is nowhere else like it on Earth. This dynamic city has developed into one of the most cosmopolitan nations in the world, which is reflected in everything from its culture and language to its architecture and food.

2 ....

One thing people often associate with Singapore is strict laws. While this may be true, Singapore enjoys one of the lowest crime rates in the world, which means that it is generally very safe for travellers and violent crime is rare. However, tourists shouldn't drop litter or chewing gum in the street or cross the road where there isn't a pedestrian crossing. If they do, they may have to pay a fine.

3 ....

You will find an endless variety of food on this multi-cultural island. The cheapest and most popular places to eat out are hawker centres, a collection of individual food stalls selling Chinese, Malay, Indian and Tamil food. The best dishes include *Mee Goreng* (fried noodles with vegetables and egg), *Laksa*, made with rice noodles in a coconut sauce with prawns, egg and chicken, and *Murtabak*, a type of spicy Indian pizza. Watch out for Singapore's most smelly food, the *durian*. This strange-looking fruit is popular with the locals, but so smelly that it is officially banned on public transport!

What is that smell? The durian.

4 ....

There is always plenty to do in Singapore, during the day and at night. Here are some of our favourite attractions.

Sentosa Island

Sentosa is a popular island resort. Its attractions include a two-kilometre long beach, an underwater world with more than 2,500 marine animals and the first 4D theatre in Southeast Asia, the *Sentosa 4D Magix*, which makes watching a film a totally interactive experience.

Relax on Sentosa beach.

G-Max reverse bungee and GX-5 Xtreme swing

For those who need a bit of adrenalin, why not try Singapore's first-ever reverse bungee? Feel what it's like to be thrown up into the sky at 200km per hour to a terrifying height of 60m. Or try the *GX-5 Xtreme swing*. This giant swing offers you the chance to experience a free fall from 50m above the Singapore River.

Night Safari

If you are looking for something to do after sunset, visit the *Night Safari*. The world's first night zoo is divided into eight different geographical zones including the Asian rainforest, African savannah and South American pampas. Explore the home of more than 900 animals on foot or by tram.

Mosaic Music Festival

This music festival began in 2005 and has since grown into one of Singapore's biggest music events. Audiences can enjoy a 10-day music experience at the Esplanade theatres, where they can listen to anything from jazz to hip hop performed by international and regional artists.

1 Culture World: Singapore

a Read the article quickly and match the headings with the paragraphs.

> Top attractions   Mouth-watering dishes
> Crimes and fines   Singapore is different

b Read the article again and answer the questions.

1 How many islands does Singapore consist of?
2 What language is only spoken in Singapore?
3 What might happen if you cross the road in the wrong place?
4 Where does the writer recommend you go to eat?
5 What are people not allowed to take on buses or trains?
6 Where can visitors watch an interactive film in 4D?
7 How can visitors travel around the night zoo?
8 How long does the Mosaic Music Festival last?

c Find the words in the article that mean ...

1 special and different from the rest (para 1)
2 an area of a road where it is safe for people to cross (para 2)
3 never seeming to finish (para 3)
4 a place where people go to rest or for sporting activities (Sentosa Island)

d Work with a partner. Answer the questions.

1 Which information interested or surprised you most about Singapore? Why?
2 Which food would / wouldn't you like to try? Why? / Why not?
3 Which attractions would / wouldn't you like to visit? Why? / Why not?

2 Your project

My country

a Work in a group. Complete a table about your country with key facts and interesting information for tourists.

Key facts	Official name: The Republic of Singapore Capital: City of Singapore Official language: Malay Other languages: English, Mandarin, Tamil Internet code: .sg
Why it's unique	cosmopolitan, multi-cultural
Tourists shouldn't ...	drop litter in the street, drop chewing gum
Tourists should try ...	food at hawker centres: Mee Goreng, Laksa, Murtabak
Top attractions	Sentosa, Night Safari, G-Max reverse bungee, Mosaic music festival

b Write an article for tourists coming to your country. Use the information in Exercise 2a to help you. Include ...

- a *Fact File* with key facts
- short paragraphs about other information in the table
- photos with captions to illustrate your article

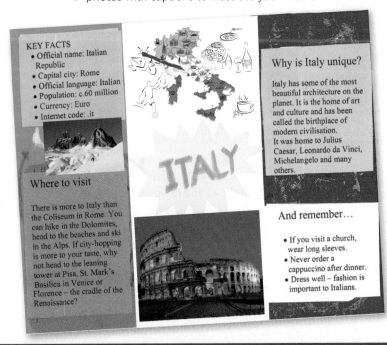

KEY FACTS
- Official name: Italian Republic
- Capital city: Rome
- Official language: Italian
- Population: c.60 million
- Currency: Euro
- Internet code: .it

Where to visit

There is more to Italy than the Coliseum in Rome. You can hike in the Dolomites, head to the beaches and ski in the Alps. If city-hopping is more to your taste, why not head to the leaning tower at Pisa, St. Mark's Basilica in Venice or Florence – the cradle of the Renaissance?

Why is Italy unique?

Italy has some of the most beautiful architecture on the planet. It is the home of art and culture and has been called the birthplace of modern civilisation. It was home to Julius Caesar, Leonardo da Vinci, Michelangelo and many others.

And remember...

- If you visit a church, wear long sleeves.
- Never order a cappuccino after dinner.
- Dress well – fashion is important to Italians.

would rather and would prefer
Third conditional
Vocabulary: Hopes and ambitions; Dependent prepositions
Interaction 12: Dealing with a problem

1 Read and listen

a Read the text quickly. Would you like to take part in a project like *Aim High*? Why? / Why not?

AIM HIGH

The decisions you make in your teenage years can shape your future. *Aim High* is an interactive online/web project that will follow a group of 12 young people as they go through a life-changing year. We'll be with the participants every step of the way … we'll see their highs and lows, their successes and frustrations.

Songwriting, football, poetry, ballet – whatever their goals and ambitions, they'll let us follow their progress through their blogs, tweets, and video diaries. You can even contact them directly to ask a question, offer advice or just have a chat. Aim High is not a competition so there are no prizes, but we expect that there will be lots of winners!

Sheila Lord, 17

Singing is my life. I really want to get a recording contract but that will depend on being discovered by a producer who likes my music. My parents would rather I went to university but I want to try and achieve my goal. Please check out my video diaries on my blog and listen to my songs. I'd love to hear your opinions!

Akilah Russell, 19

I aim to become a top journalist. I'm doing some work experience at our local newspaper offices, but in the future I'd rather work in television than for a newspaper. I want to follow my dream and succeed in what I do. Over-ambitious? I'd rather not think about that! Maybe I am, but look at my blog and let me know what you think.

Tom Muggleton, 18

My goals are to get into university, to live away from home for the first time and to make some new friends. These are huge challenges for me because I'm quite shy. Sometimes I think I'd prefer not to go; I'd rather stay at home. Then I remember how exciting this year is going to be. If you want to contact me, please visit my blog.

b 🔊 3.29 Read the text again and listen. Are the sentences *right* (✓), *wrong* (✗) or *doesn't say* (–)?

1 The *Aim High* participants are all 18 years old.
2 Viewers can interact with the participants on their blogs.
3 Sheila would prefer to go to university.
4 Akilah isn't sure about what she wants to do in the future.
5 Tom thinks the year ahead is going to be easy.
6 Viewers can give their opinions.

c Find the words in the text that mean …

1 decide or influence something (para 1)
2 things that you want to achieve (para 2)
3 look at something to see what it is like (para 3)
4 very good or very important (para 4)

d Work in a group. Answer the questions.

1 Which of the three participants you read about would be the most interesting to follow? Why?
2 What are your goals and ambitions for next year?

2 Grammar

would rather and *would prefer*

a Read the examples. Then (circle) the correct words to complete the rules.

> ⤷ ***I'd rather work*** *in television* ***than*** *for a newspaper.*
> ***My parents would rather I went*** *to university.*
> ***I'd rather not think*** *about that!*
> ***I'd prefer not to go; I'd rather stay*** *at home.*

- We use *would rather* and *would prefer* to express our preferences **in general** / **in a specific situation**.
- *Would rather (not)* is followed by the infinitive **with** / **without** *to*.
- *Would prefer (not)* is followed by the infinitive **with** / **without** *to*.
- We use *would rather* + someone + **present** / **past** to say what we would like someone else to do.
- We use **than** / **that** to express a preference between two options.

Grammar reference: Workbook page 100

b Complete the sentences with *prefer* or *rather*.

1 I'd .... play games than watch TV.
2 My parents would .... I went to the local college.
3 Would you .... to watch a horror film or a romantic comedy?
4 Sheila would .... go trekking for her holiday than sit on a beach.
5 I'd much .... live in a student residence than in a flat on my own.

c Complete the sentences so they are true for you, then compare your answers with a partner.

1 Instead of being in class right now I'd rather be ....
2 I've got to .... this evening but I'd prefer to ... .

3 Vocabulary

Hopes and ambitions

a 🔊 **3.30** Read the definitions and complete the examples with the words. Then listen and check.

| achieve | ~~aim~~ | ambition | challenge |
| expect | goal | hope | |

1 intend: *I* __aim__ *to be a millionaire one day.*
2 a strong wish to be successful: *She's got a lot of* ....
3 an aim or purpose: *Our* .... *is to win the league this season.*
4 something difficult that needs a lot of effort: *Running a marathon is a real* ....
5 succeed in finishing something or reaching an aim: *I want to* .... *my dreams.*
6 to want something to happen: *I want this job, so I* .... *the interview goes well.*
7 to think something will probably happen: *I* .... *that you'll pass the exam because you're good at Maths.*

> ### Check it out!
>
> - To talk about what you want to happen in the future we use *hope*, not *wish*.
>   I **hope** I will pass my driving test on Saturday.
>   NOT ~~I wish I will pass my driving test on Saturday~~.

b (Circle) the correct words.

1 There's a lot of competition, so it's going to be *a challenge / an aim* to get a job in advertising.
2 I *expect / hope* he'll get the job as he's got more experience than me.
3 He *hopes / achieves* to go to university next year.
4 My biggest *aim / achievement* last year was winning the gold award for skating.
5 Things that are *ambitious / challenging* are very difficult.

c Work in a group. Answer the questions.

1 What do you hope to do when you're older?
2 What decisions do you need to make now that will shape your future?

4 Speak

a Work in a group. Add two more activities to each circle. Then ask and answer questions to find out which are the most popular activities.

⟶ A: *Would you rather do your homework, go shopping or play video games after school today?*

B: *I'd much rather go shopping than do my homework!*

C: *I'd prefer to play video games.*

do my homework   go shopping

After school today

play video games

go to the cinema

This weekend

go to a party   stay at home

do a job I love   do a job that pays well

In the future

start my own business

b Work in a group. Do you agree or disagree with the statements? Why? / Why not?

1 At my age it's difficult to decide what to do in the future.

2 Parents should let their children make the important decisions in their lives.

5 Listen

a 🔊 3.31 Listen to three people talking about how they celebrated the end of the school year. Match the people with the pictures. Write *E* (Ellen), *P* (Pablo) or *M* (Mario).

A

B

C

b 🔊 3.31 Listen again and answer the questions.

1 What did the students wear to the prom?

2 What was the only disappointment about the prom?

3 How long was the trip to London?

4 What did the speaker lose on the trip to London?

5 What was the weather like on the last day of Mario's exams?

6 Why was it a double celebration for Mario and his classmates?

c Work with a partner. Answer the questions.

1 Which of the three end-of-school celebrations would you prefer to take part in? Why?

2 What might you do to celebrate the end of school?

Culture Vulture

Did you know that at the end of a school year many schools in the USA produce a *yearbook*? It contains photos and articles about the year. Every student gets a copy. Do you have yearbooks in your country? Do you think they are a nice way to remember your school years? Why? / Why not?

6 Grammar

Third conditional

a Look at the examples. Then (circle) the correct words to complete the rules.

> ⟶ *If the weather **had been** better, we **would have had** our photos taken in the garden.*
> *If I **hadn't lost** my camera, it **would have been** the perfect trip!*
> *How **would** you **have felt** if you **had won** the World Cup?*
> *If we**'d visited** London before our exam, we **could have got** better marks!*

- We can use the third conditional to talk about imaginary situations that **happened** / **didn't happen** in the past.
- The third conditional is formed with *if* + **past perfect** / **present perfect**, + *would have* + past participle.
- When the *if* clause is positive, it means the action **did** / **didn't** take place.
- When the *if* clause is negative, it means the action **did** / **didn't** take place.
- We can use **could** / **can** instead of *would*.

Grammar reference: Workbook page 88

> ### Check it out!
>
> - We never use *if* + *would* in the same clause in conditional sentences.
>   *If we had lost the match, we would have been unhappy.* NOT ~~If we would have lost the match, we would have been unhappy.~~

b Read the sentences and answer the questions.

1 If my phone hadn't broken, I would have called you.
   - Did my phone break? Did I call you?
2 She would have stayed for lunch if she'd had time.
   - Did she stay for lunch? Did she have time?
3 His mum wouldn't have got cross if he'd told the truth.
   - Did his mum get cross? Did he tell the truth?
4 He wouldn't have been late if he hadn't overslept.
   - Was he late? Did he oversleep?

c Rewrite the sentences using the third conditional. The first one is done for you.

1 I didn't drive slowly. The police stopped me.
   If I had driven slowly, the police wouldn't have stopped me .
2 I stayed up late. I felt exhausted the next day.
   If I hadn't _____ .
3 She didn't read his email carefully. She didn't see his good news.
   If she _____ .
4 The bus was late. They missed the beginning of the film.
   If the bus _____ .
5 We didn't take a taxi. We didn't have any money.
   We would _____ .
6 They didn't wait for half an hour outside the stadium so they didn't see Messi.
   They would _____ .

d Work with a partner. Answer the questions.

1 What would you have done today if you hadn't come to school?
2 If you'd been born fifty years ago, how would your life have been different?

7 Pronunciation ⏺D·V·D

Sentence stress

a 🔊 3.32 Listen to the sentences and underline the words that are stressed.

1 I'm really interested in learning about technology.
2 He's looking forward to starting university.
3 It'll depend on his marks, but he wants to be a doctor.
4 What do you think about the new series of *Aim High*?

b What types of words are stressed? What types are unstressed?

c Underline the stressed words in the sentence.

It depends on the weather, but I think I'll probably go to the beach at the weekend.

d 🔊 3.33 Listen, check and repeat.

(8) Vocabulary

Dependent prepositions

a Some verbs and adjectives are often followed by a preposition. Write the words in the correct columns. Sometimes more than one answer is possible.

Verbs
concentrate   decide   depend   look forward
make progress   succeed

Adjectives
bad   good   interested   keen

on	in	at	to

b 🔊 **3.34** Complete the sentences with the correct words. Then listen and check.

1 Are you .... in art?
2 I hope you .... in getting a place at the best university.
3 She's really .... at history. She failed the last exam.
4 Are you .... to going on holiday? I can't wait!
5 I can't .... on this film while you're talking on the phone.
6 I'm sure he'll .... on a medical career if he can.
7 The teacher asked me if I was .... in English.
8 I don't know what we'll do at the weekend. It .... on the weather.

c Work with a partner. Answer the questions.

1 What things are you interested in? What things are you good at?
2 What have you succeeded in doing this year?
3 What are you looking forward to?

> ### Check it out!
>
> • *Looking forward to* is always followed by the **-ing** form of the verb.
> I'm looking forward to **finishing** the class.
> NOT ~~I'm looking forward to finish the class.~~

Interaction 12 (DVD)

Dealing with a problem

a 🔊 **3.35** Rosa, Peter and Carlos are organising the end-of-year party at school. Listen to the conversation. What's the problem? How do they plan to solve it?

b 🔊 **3.35** Listen again and tick (✓) the expressions you hear.

Telling others about the problem

You're not going to believe this. ☐
There's a bit of a problem with … ☐
We've got a huge problem! ☐

Blame and regret

It's (not) your fault. ☐
I told you so! ☐
If we hadn't .... , this wouldn't have happened. ☐

Looking for solutions

OK, so what are we going to do now? ☐
We'll sort this out. ☐
Let's make a plan. ☐
That might work. ☐

c Work with a partner.
Student A: Turn to page 120.
Student B: Turn to page 123.

Portfolio 12

A record of achievement

a Look at Anita's Record of achievement and answer the questions.

1 What has she got better at?
2 What does she still need to work on?
3 Did she achieve her goals this year?
4 What are her aims for next year?

Record of Achievement   **Name:** *Anita Gupta*

Think about your progress in English during the last year. How good are you at the following? Mark yourself on the line from *W* (weak) to *S* (strong).

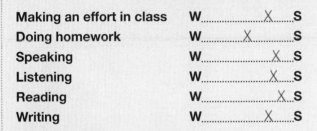

Making an effort in class	W................X.....S
Doing homework	W.........X.........S
Speaking	W...................X..S
Listening	W................X...S
Reading	W.............X..S
Writing	W..........X....S

Which activities did you most enjoy?

I liked working in groups best. I enjoyed the activities where we worked together. I don't like working on my own very much.

Which activities helped you make progress in English this year?

I think that the speaking activities have helped me most this year. Last year I wasn't very confident at speaking in English but this year we have practised a lot. Also I now have a friend from Australia so I practise English with him.

Have you achieved your goals this year?

My goal for this year was to pass all the subjects and I've just found out that I have! I think I could have made better progress in English if I'd worked a little bit harder but I feel that I have improved.

What are your aims for next term?

Next term I aim to do more of the homework. This year I haven't done all the homework and I know I will get a worse mark because of that.

What will you need to do next term to help you achieve your aims?

I will try to organise my time better so I can do my homework.

If you had planned the course, what would you have done differently?

I would have liked to watch a film in English as part of the course and if I had planned the course, I would have done less grammar and more speaking!

Is there anything that you are able to do now that you couldn't do at the beginning of the course?

When I listen to music in English, I can sometimes understand the lyrics! At the beginning of the course I couldn't do that. It depends on the song – some are still really difficult, but I feel that I am able to understand more.

---

b Read the record of achievement again carefully. <u>Underline</u> examples of the following:

1 the past simple
2 the present perfect with *just*
3 the third conditional
4 a future tense
5 two ways of expressing ability
6 two verbs or adjectives with dependent prepositions

c Write your own record of achievement in your notebook. Try and use a variety of tenses with at least one example of those in Exercise b. Answer with as much information as you can.

d Work with a partner. Read your partner's record of achievement and offer him/her some advice.

It Ain't Over 'Til It's Over

1 Song

a 🔊 **3.36** Listen to the beginning of the song and number the lines, 1–4. Then (circle) what the song is about.

So much time, wasted ☐

Here we are, still together ☐

Playing games with love ☐

We are one ... ☐

The song is about being ...

with friends   in love   at home

b 🔊 **3.37** Listen to the next part of the song and complete the lines with the words.

alive   cried   over   over   pain   tried

So many tears I've ....

So much .... inside

But baby it ain't over 'til it's ....

So many years we've ....

To keep our love ....

But baby it ain't over 'til it's ....

c 🔊 **3.38** Listen to part of the song and (circle) the correct words.

How many *days / times*

Did we *give / take* up

But we always *worked / sorted* things out

And all my doubts and *fears / questions*

Kept me wondering, yeah

If I'd always, always be *your friend / in love*

d 🔊 **3.39** Listen to the whole song. Then answer the questions.

1 Are the people in the song together now?

2 What do they wish?

 A They hadn't stayed together.

 B They had been happier together in the past.

 C They had wasted more time and played more games.

3 '*It ain't over 'til it's over*' was famously said by American baseball player and coach, Yogi Berra, when his team played very badly. What does it mean?

(2) Sound check

a Match the contractions with the full forms.

'cause 'til ain't | because is not until

b 🔊 **3.40** Listen and count the syllables.
But baby it ain't over 'til it's over
1 How many syllables are in the line?
2 Why do we use contractions in songs?

(3) Musical notes
The 1990s

Rap

Lenny Kravitz

The 1990s

The song *It Ain't Over 'Til It's Over* is by the American singer-songwriter Lenny Kravitz. His music, incorporating different styles such as rock and reggae, became very popular in the 1990s. Other music styles that were popular in the 1990s included pop and alternative rock. People also listened to R&B and rap music, which came to Britain from the US.

Pop

Alternative rock

R&B

a 🔊 **3.41** Listen and number the types of music from the 1990s in the order you hear them.

b Rank the four styles of music in order 1–4, from the one you like most, to the one you like least. Compare with a partner and explain why you like or dislike each style.

R&B .... Rap ....

Alternative rock ....

Pop ....

Review 11 and 12

1 Grammar

a Complete the subject or object questions.

1 Mr Harmer teaches ICT at school.
Who .... ?

2 Most bank robberies take place on Fridays.
When .... ?

3 My brother went to a concert last night.
Who .... ?

4 The thieves stole an expensive painting from the museum.
What .... ?

5 Lucy updates her social networking site every day.
Who .... ?

6 Harry organised a trip to London to celebrate the end of the school year.
What .... ? ☐ 6

b Rewrite the sentences with *wish* or *if only*.

1 Alesha can't dance, but she would like to.
She ....

2 Adi didn't revise for his exams and he failed everything.
If ....

3 Anika wants to have long hair.
She ....

4 Manuel and Gabi want to live by the sea.
If ....

5 Diana doesn't want her dad to smoke.
She ....

6 Henri's parents don't let him go out during the week. He wants to go out on Tuesday.
He .... ☐ 6

c Circle the correct words.

1 If she *hadn't cheated / didn't cheat* in the exam, she wouldn't *get / have got* into trouble.

2 If I *had chosen / would choose* a safer password, no one would *hack / have hacked* into my social networking site.

3 The vandals *had gone / would have gone* to prison if they *had been / would be* caught.

4 We *had had / would have had* a school prom if the head teacher *had / would have* let us.

5 If he *had / hadn't* lost his passport, he could *go / have gone* on the school trip.

6 He could *go / have gone* to university if he *had / would have* got better grades at school. ☐ 6

d Complete the sentences for each situation.

1 Your friend wants to order a mushroom pizza to share with you. You don't like mushroom, but you like ham and pineapple.
I'd rather ....

2 Your friends want to meet at 6 o'clock. You want to meet at 7 o'clock.
I'd rather we ....

3 Jack wants to watch the sports channel. Lucia wants to watch the movie channel.
She'd prefer ....

4 Your mum asks you if you want to go into town or stay at home.
Would you prefer .... ?

5 You want to leave school and get a job. Your parents want you to go to university.
They'd rather ....

6 Students can study Spanish or Italian at school. You want to study Italian.
You'd prefer .... ☐ 6

e Complete the second sentence so that it means the same as the first.

1 I wish I hadn't gone to the party.
If only .... !

2 I don't want to get a job this summer, but I have to.
I wish ....

3 They would have gone out to celebrate if they'd known it was Dan's birthday.
They .... stayed at home if .... Dan's birthday.

4 If she had revised more, she wouldn't have failed her exams.
She would have ....

5 He'd rather do his homework on the computer.
He'd prefer ....

6 I don't want you to tell her the secret.
I'd rather .... ☐ 6

How are you doing?

How many points have you got? Put two crosses on the chart: one for grammar and one for vocabulary.

	1	2	3	4	5	6	7	8	9	10	11	12	13
Grammar													

	1	2	3	4	5	6	7	8	9	10	11	12	13
Vocabulary													

② Vocabulary

ⓐ Complete the crossword.

Across

1 a person who steals something from a shop
4 break into someone's house and take things
5 get into someone's computer system
8 copying someone else's work and saying it's yours

Down

2 stealing personal information to commit a crime
3 take something that isn't yours
4 a person who steals money from a bank
6 a person who writes graffiti or breaks things
7 copying software or music from the internet | 9 |

ⓑ Complete the crime collocations.

1 c_____ a crime
2 arrest a s_____
3 c_____ someone with a crime
4 g_____ to prison
5 a prison s_____
6 pay a f_____
7 community s_____
8 have a criminal r_____ | 8 |

GREEN:	Great! Tell your teacher your score!
YELLOW:	Not bad, but go to the website for extra practice.
RED:	Talk to your teacher and look at Units 11 and 12 again. Go to the website for extra practice.

| 14 | 15 | 16 | 17 | 18 | 19 | 20 | 21 | 22 | 23 | 24 | 25 | 26 | 27 | 28 | 29 | 30 |

| 14 | 15 | 16 | 17 | 18 | 19 | 20 | 21 | 22 | 23 | 24 | 25 | 26 | 27 | 28 | 29 | 30 |

ⓒ Complete the table with the words (1–6) for the verbs and adjectives.

noun	verb	adjective
aim	1	–
expectation	2	–
achievement	3	–
4	–	ambitious
5	–	challenging
6	–	hopeful

| 6 |

ⓓ Complete the sentences with the correct preposition: *on*, *in*, *at* or *to*.

1 We may go. It depends _____ the weather.
2 They're interested _____ learning Chinese.
3 Did he succeed _____ finding a job?
4 I wish I was better _____ playing the drums.
5 I need to concentrate _____ revising now.
6 I'm looking forward _____ my birthday.
7 She's very keen _____ the idea.

| 7 |

Correct it!

Correct these typical learner errors from Units 11 and 12.

1 I wish I would find my pen.
....
2 One night she decided to stole the painting.
....
3 The most common age for a person to make a crime is between 16 and 22.
....
4 I rather listen to music than play games on the computer.
....
5 I would prefere to stay in the Abrahams hotel.
....
6 I wish you can come to my birthday party next week.
....
7 I didn't expected to get the first prize.
....
8 We are looking to hearing from you soon.
....
9 But it depends of where you live.
....
10 I am very interested to become part of this project.
....

Skills 4 Real
UNITS 1–4

① Speaking

a Which are important qualities for a good friend? Put the following in order from the most important to the least important.

generous   patient   fun   understanding
good sense of humour   kind

b Do you agree with your partner? Why? / Why not?

c Work with a partner. Answer the questions.
Have you ever …
1 told a friend how important he/she is to you?
2 fallen out with a friend and never made up?
3 felt bad about how you have spoken to a friend?
4 done anything dangerous to help a friend?

A As It Comes To An End
by Kay

As I sit here in class,
I observe my friends
And look forward to the year
Coming to an end.

It's gonna be sad
To say goodbye.
I'll miss everyone.
I know I will cry.
I remember the day
When I came back
To be with my friends
And get on the right track.

We had so many moments;
Some bad, most great.
I'll always remember the love
And erase the hate.

I don't wanna say goodbye
To all my friends.
I don't want this year
To come to an end.

B The Perfect Friend
by Shannen Wrass

Today I found a friend
who knew everything I felt
she knew my weakness
and the problems I've been dealt.
She understood my wonders
and listened to my dreams,
she listened to how I felt about
  life and love
and knew what it all means.
Not once did she interrupt me
or tell me I was wrong
she understood what I was going
  through
and promised she'd stay long.
I reached out to this friend,
to show her that I care
to pull her close and let her know
how much I need her there.
I went to hold her hand
to pull her a bit nearer
and I realized this perfect friend
  I found
was nothing but a mirror.

E 'A brother may not be a friend, but a friend will always be a brother.'
Samuel Richardson

C Ode To A Chatroom
by Marie Lehmkuhl

One day I decided to get on the net,
I thought a chat room would be my best bet.
I saw names and words come up from where
I knew not.
I soon took a chance and had a nice thought,
Could I do this, it looked really neat.
I saw names on the screen that started with sweet,
sweet smiles, Jo, and Smokey were there too,
And then I saw it, 'Oh, yes, we're talking to you,
come on in and chat for a while.'
And when I did I started to smile.
I saw Chuckie and Robbie and soon I was friends
with quite a few people by the day's end.
And after awhile they called me their friend.
Sometimes I come in and my friends are not there,
But I'll go back again because I know that they care.
Some live in the States and some do not,
But they always know when I need to talk.
I am so glad I took the leap and went into the
chat room where friends are so neat.

D Purple Ronnie Poems:
I want to tell you something
It's soppy but it's true
If friendship grew like flowers
I know that I'd pick YOU

F 'Books and friends should be few but good.'

② Reading

a Look at the poems and quotes about friendship. Where do you think you would find them?

b Read the poems and quotes quickly. Which one (A–F) is about somebody who …

1 is about to leave school?
2 has just discovered the possibility of making online friends?
3 is getting to know themselves better?
4 believes that it's better to have one or two really good friends than lots of average friends?
5 may get on better with a friend than a member of their family?

c Read the poems and quotes again. Are the statements *right* (✓), *wrong* (✗) or *doesn't say* (–)?

1 The author of poem A only has happy memories of her school days.
2 The author of poem B believes you should be your own friend.
3 The author of poem C isn't enjoying making friends online.
4 The author of poem D wants to tell their friend that they are appreciated.
5 The author of quote E believes you automatically get on well with your family.
6 The author of quote F has lots of good friends.

d Match the words with the meanings.

1 erase ☐
2 an ode ☐
3 neat ☐
4 a leap ☐
5 weakness ☐
6 soppy ☐

A good (informal US)
B remove information
C a quality or part of someone that is not good
D a poem expressing the writer's feelings
E a large jump
F showing or feeling too much emotion

e Work with a partner. Which poem or quote do you like best? Why?

③ Listening

Helen

Simone

Llorenç

a ◁)) 3.42 Listen to three people talking about their best friends. Match the opinions with the speakers.

1 We've known each other since we were three or four.

....

2 I love my best friends sense of humour.

....

3 We have lots of the same friends.

....

b ◁)) 3.42 Listen again. What three questions does the interviewer ask? Take notes on the speakers' answers.

1 ....
2 ....
3 ....

c Work with a partner. Compare your notes and ask and answer the questions in Exercise 3b together.

④ Writing

a You are going to write a very short poem or a quote about friends and friendship, to include in your friend's birthday card.

● Think of a friend (real or imaginary) that you can write about.
● How does your friend make you feel? What is special about him/her?
● Is your poem or quote going to be funny or serious?
● Make a note of useful words and ideas.
● Write your poem or quote.

b Work in a group. Read your poems and quotes to each other. Do you like them? Why? / Why not?

Skills 4 Real
UNITS 5–8

① Speaking

a Work with a partner. Imagine you are a musician. How many ways of becoming famous can you think of?

b Compare your ideas with another pair. Who has more ideas?

Writing a great song is only half the battle. How do you become a household name? Steve O'Rourke and Stuart Plant offer sound advice.

How to get your music heard

Lily Allen has come a long, long way from her MySpace beginnings

1 Get social

It worked for Lily Allen and the Arctic Monkeys and it might just work for you. Facebook allows easy-to-design fan sites and artist pages, although cross promotion can be tricky. And you need to Tweet to stay in touch with fans.

2 Get played and paid

Online music stores like cdbaby.com specialise in selling music from independent artists. They sell your music in both CD and digital format (including an iTunes listing) for low start-up costs. It's how people like Jack Johnson started out.

3 Festival focus

The UK has been in festival frenzy with many major events desperately looking for new talent to fill secondary stages. Check out the website www.efestivals.co.uk to find out what's on, where, and who you need to approach.

4 Give it away now

Unlike MySpace songs, SoundCloud.com songs can be embedded anywhere. It has no file-size limit and it lets fans comment on specific parts of a recording. Quicker and easier than MySpace – just not as popular … Yet.

5 Hey Mr DJ!

There are two types of radio DJ – those that play from a playlist and those that break new music. Ignore the former and focus on the latter. It's easy to find contact details via MySpace or Facebook, then just send a high-quality MP3 (192kbps).

6 Think about the audience

Many unknown musicians get their music heard by having tracks published in videogames. Visit gamespress.com and check out the contact details for hundreds of games publishers and developers.

7 Show what you're made of

If you want to impress a particular label or artist, remix an official track and send it to the management. This recently happened with the Dandy Warhols – resulting in the remix being included in their next official release.

8 Spend a little money and a lot of time

Nothing is better than physical contact with potential fans. Bulk-buy CDs, burn your best tracks, scribble your band's URL, then give out to punters at the kind of gig that fits your music. Simple but effective.

9 Got the X-Factor?

Check out community sites such as Garageband.com for talent competitions that can result in a chart listing and even being played on 400 FM radio stations.

10 Get creative

Stickers are cool. Stickers with your band's name and logo are even cooler. Visit www.bandstickers.co.uk where you can get 1,000 custom-designed stickers for £150.

② Reading

a Read the text quickly. How many of your ideas from Exercise 1 were mentioned?

b Read the text again and answer the questions.

1 What do musicians use social networking sites like Facebook for?
2 If you want to sell your music online, which website can help you?
3 Which website can help you if you want to perform your music live?
4 How can you contact radio DJs to get them to play your music?
5 Apart from social networking sites, what's one popular way for new musicians to get published?
6 What can you do to show a record label that you have musical ability?
7 How can talent competitions be useful?
8 What two things could you give away to potential fans?

c Match the words or phrases with the meanings.

1 a household name ☐
2 approach ☐
3 the former … the latter ☐
4 release ☐
5 scribble ☐
6 punter ☐

A speak or write to someone
B a CD or piece of music that is published
C a very famous person
D write down quickly
E someone who buys products
F the first … the second

d Work with a partner. Answer the questions.

1 Do you think the advice in the text is good? Why? / Why not?
2 If you had a band, which of the things would you do?
3 Can you think of any other ways to get your music heard?
4 What are the advantages and disadvantages of being a 'household name'?

③ Listening

David Andrea Mick

a 🔊 **3.43** Listen to three people talking about music. Match the phrases with the speakers.

1 I'm really into pop music. ....
2 I've always got a song in my head. ....
3 I play the piano and the drums. ....

b 🔊 **3.43** Listen again. What three questions does the interviewer ask? Take notes on the speakers' answers.

1 ....
2 ....
3 ....

c Work with a partner. Compare your notes ask and answer the questions in Exercise 3b together.

④ Writing

a Work with a partner. You're going to write some tips for doing something successfully. Write about one of the ideas in the box or your own idea.

How to …

> take photos   dress like a top model
> play football/basketball
> design a website   speak English fluently
> come top in your exams

b Write your tips (6–8). Include:

1 a heading for each tip
2 imperatives (*Visit …, Check out …*) or modals of ability (*You can …, You could …*)
3 useful website addresses

c Swap your tips with another pair. Is the advice useful?

1 Speaking

Work with a partner. Answer the questions.

1 Which museums and art galleries are popular in your country? Have you visited any of them?
2 Do you think objects like T-shirts, watches or bags can be forms of art? Why? / Why not?
3 Which well-known artists and designers come from your country? Do you like their work? Why? / Why not?

The Pop Artist/Designer

File Edit View Insert Format Tools Actions Help

http://interactive.cambridge.org/

Tate Modern brings together artists from the 1980s onwards who have embraced commerce and the mass media to build their own 'brands'.

'Good business is the best art,' Andy Warhol famously remarked. Since his death in 1987, many subsequent artists have followed his lead.

A number of the artists featured in the Pop Life exhibition have explored the boundaries between art and commerce and the roles of artists and designers. We've selected just a few to get you thinking about your own design ideas.

THE POP ARTIST/DESIGNER

Keith Haring

Artists such as Keith Haring created signature designs and products such as toys, magnets and T-shirts. The exhibition will include a reconstruction of Keith Haring's Pop Shop (right).

In 1986, Haring opened his Pop Shop in New York, offering a range of merchandise branded with his distinct visual style. The walls, floor and ceiling were covered with Haring's graffiti, and the goods on sale changed hands to the accompaniment of a continuous rap soundtrack.

Takashi Murakami

There will also be an exciting new commission by the Japanese artist Takashi Murakami. Murakami has worked across different media and disciplines including painting, giant inflatable sculptures and performance events. He has also designed everything from key chains, mouse pads, plush dolls, T-shirts to Louis Vuitton handbags.

Murakami's retrospective at the Museum of Contemporary Art in Los Angeles, for example, incorporated a Louis Vuitton boutique in the middle of the exhibition, selling merchandise that the artist had designed for the fashion label.

The YBAs

There will also be a gallery dedicated to the so-called 'Young British Artists', which will include ephemera from Tracey Emin and Sarah Lucas's shop.

As part of the YBA generation, Tracey Emin and Sarah Lucas opened 'The Shop' in 1993, a project created for marketing their work. For six months they rented a space, formerly a doctor's surgery, in east London's Bethnal Green Road, where they made and sold solo and collaborative work.

DESIGN CHALLENGE

The challenge was to use the Pop Life exhibition and featured art and artists as inspiration to create an original Pop-inspired T-shirt design.

'The artists shown in the Pop Life exhibition at the Tate Modern inspired this T-shirt entitled 'Pop Life Deserves A Toast'. Displays by pop icons such as Keith Haring and Takashi Murakami influenced the customisation and colour. The toasters symbolise the everyday consumer product, along with the toast that pops up representing the energy and lifestyle of Pop Art that we all know and love.'

Young Tate Winning Design: *Pop Life Deserves A Toast* by Kayleigh Doughty

② Reading

a Look at the information about the *Pop Life* exhibition. What is the exhibition about?

b Read the information quickly. Which artist …

> Andy Warhol   Keith Haring
> Takashi Murakami   Tracey Emin
> Kayleigh Doughty

1 won a competition with a T-shirt design?
2 said that business was good for art?
3 sold fashion products during his/her exhibition?
4 opened a shop in London with another artist?
5 designed toys, magnets and T-shirts?

c Read the information again. Are the sentences *right* (✓), *wrong* (✗) or *doesn't say* (–)?

1 The *Pop Life* exhibition looks at the connection between art and business.
2 Haring's Pop Shop sold music products.
3 Murakami never paints.
4 Tracey Emin and Sarah Lucas only had 'The Shop' for a few months.
5 The winning T-shirt in the Pop Life Design Challenge was inspired by classical art.

d Match the words with the meanings.

1 commerce
2 boundaries
3 merchandise
4 boutique
5 icons
6 symbolise

A famous people admired by others
B limits
C business
D represent
E shop
F things that are bought and sold

e Work with a partner. Answer the questions.

1 Would you like to visit the *Pop Life* exhibition? Why? / Why not?
2 Do you think artists should sell products as part of their exhibitions? Why? / Why not?

③ Listening

Kristin

Sarah

Seamus

a 🔊 **3.44** Listen to three people talking about museum exhibitions. Match the phrases with the speakers.

1 I prefer history museums to art museums.
....
2 I like museums with interactive exhibits.
....
3 I went to an exhibition at my favourite football club recently. ....

b 🔊 **3.44** Listen again. What three questions does the interviewer ask? Take notes on the speakers' answers.

1 ....
2 ....
3 ....

c Work with a partner. Compare your notes ask and answer the questions in Exercise 3b together.

④ Writing

a Write a review for your blog of an exhibition which is on in your city or country now. Include this information:

● the theme of the exhibition
● what you can see there (photographs, paintings, objects, etc.)
● the artists
● the venue, dates, ticket prices
● your opinion of the exhibition

b Work in a group. Swap information about the exhibitions. Which exhibition would you most like to go to? Why?

Interaction: Student A

Interaction 1   page 8

c   Have conversations with your partner. First, ask questions to find out your partner's news. Then answer your partner's questions about your news (you invent the details). Use the Interaction language to help you.

Conversation 1: You haven't done much recently. Your cousin has got married. You failed your Maths and Science exams and your dad's broken his leg.

Conversation 2: You've been to watch a really good film at the cinema and you've bought some new trainers. You've started exercise classes too.

d   Have a conversation about your real news. Use the Interaction language to help you.

Interaction 2   page 16

d   Take turns being the customer and the shop assistant. First, you are the customer. Return these items to the shop. Then respond to your partner when he/she is the customer. Use the Interaction language to help you.

Interaction 3   page 26

c   You are going on a four-day trip to a music festival in Scotland. You will be camping at the festival. Decide together what you are going to take with you in your rucksacks. Use the Interaction language to help you.

Extra information about the trip

- Scotland is famous for having a lot of mosquitoes.
- There aren't many shops in the area. The nearest town is 4km away.
- It rains a lot in Scotland.

Interaction 4   page 34

d   Tell your partner about your problem. Listen to your partner's advice and accept or reject it. Then listen to your partner's problem and give advice. Use the Interaction language to help you.

Your problem: You are worried about a friend of yours. He/She has just got a motorbike and he/she always drives too fast and in a dangerous way. He/She thinks it's funny to race through the town centre but you're worried he'll/she'll have an accident soon.

Interaction 5   page 44

c Work with a partner. Discuss what different things make a school better. You can use the ideas in the box, but add some of your own ideas.

> a theatre   a laptop for every student   a music studio   good science labs
> a café with relaxing music   a swimming pool

d Now work in your group of four. Decide on the two most important things to include in a new school. Interrupt the other people in the group if necessary. Use the Interaction language to help you.

Interaction 6   page 52

c You are going to take part in three debates. Before you start, write down some ideas to support your opinions. During the debates use the Interaction language to help you agree and disagree.

1 Reality TV is great television. You agree. Your partner disagrees.

2 Being famous is wonderful. You disagree. Your partner agrees.

3 Hard work is more important than natural talent. You agree. Your partner disagrees.

d Have a discussion about the topics with your real opinions.

Interaction 7   page 62

c Laura, a girl in your class, hasn't come to school for the last three days. Your partner is a friend of Laura's and he/she will help you guess what might have happened to her. Use the Interaction language to help you.

d There was a big party at the weekend, but your friend Kevin didn't go. Your partner is going to guess what happened. Tell him/her if his/her ideas might be right. Use the Interaction language to help you.

You know that:

Kevin gets on very well with the boy who had the party.

A girl he likes was going to the party.

You saw him the day of the party and he was fine.

He was going to play football just before the party.

He had a big argument with his brother the day before the party.

His older cousin had a party the same night.

Interaction 8   page 70

c Look at the descriptions of the gadgets below and think about how they might work. Then explain to your partner how to use the gadgets and answer any questions he/she has. Use the Interaction language to help you.

● A gadget to make learning English easier.

● A gadget to help with the housework.

d Now listen to your partner's explanations of how to use two gadgets. Ask for more information if you don't understand the explanations. Use the Interaction language to help you.

Interaction 9   page 80

c Look at the information and act out the conversations with your partner. Use the Interaction language to help you.

Conversation 1: Your friend has bought some new clothes and asks you if you like them. You think they're awful (you decide why), but you don't want to hurt his/her feelings so you tell some white lies to be tactful. Your partner starts the conversation.

Conversation 2: You have bought your friend a present (you decide what). You think it's great, but you're not sure if he/she likes it. Ask him/her if he/she likes the present. You start the conversation.

Interaction 10   page 88

c You are going to an Arts Festival together next weekend. You need to check some details. Use the Interaction language to help you.

Student A

	Saturday		Sunday	
Morning	**What?**	A presentation of new computer games	**What?**	
	Where?	....	**Where?**	....
	Cost?	Free	**Cost?**	£2.50
Afternoon	**What?**	....	**What?**	Winners of short film competition
	Where?	New Theatre	**Where?**	....
	Cost?	....	**Cost?**	....
Evening	**What?**	Rock concert – lots of different bands	**What?**	....
	Where?	....	**Where?**	The Queen's Hall
	Cost?	£35	**Cost?**	Free

Interaction 11   page 98

c Look at the information and act out the conversations with your partner. Use the Interaction language to help you.

Conversation 1: You are a teacher and one of your students borrowed the class video camera for some project work. He/She took it home to use and now it's broken. Talk to the student and decide on what should happen. Your partner starts the conversation.

Conversation 2: You didn't go to one of your classes yesterday because you had an important exam and you hadn't studied for it (you decide on the subject and why you hadn't studied). Your teacher wants to talk to you. Apologise and explain why you didn't go to the class. You start the conversation.

Interaction 12   page 106

c Look at the information and act out the conversations with your partner. Try to find solutions to the problems. Use the Interaction language to help you.

Conversation 1: You are working on a school project together. You had all the information saved on your laptop and it has just broken. You have lost the whole project! You think that your friend Jack, who's a computer genius, will be able to repair the laptop and find the project.

Conversation 2: You are preparing an outdoor party to celebrate the end of the school year. The party is in three days' time. The weather forecast predicts rain and storms. You want to cancel the party completely! It will be a disaster in the rain.

Interaction: Student B

Interaction 1   page 8

c   Have conversations with your partner. First, answer your partner's questions about your news (you invent the details). Then ask questions to find out your partners news. Use the Interaction language to help you.

Conversation 1: You've started singing lessons and you've been to a concert. You're training for a marathon.

Conversation 2: You haven't done much recently. You've got into a very good sports team but you're a bit worried because you don't know anyone on the team.

d   Have a conversation about your real news. Use the Interaction language to help you.

Interaction 2   page 16

d   Take turns being the customer and the shop assistant. First, respond to your partner when he/she is the customer. Then you are the customer. Return these items to the shop. Use the Interaction language to help you.

RECEIPT
Rucksack
February 4th

Hand-held console bought last month

Interaction 3   page 26

c   You are going on a four-day trip to a music festival in Scotland. You will be camping at the festival. Decide together what you are going to take with you in your rucksacks. Use the Interaction language to help you.

Extra information about the trip

- The sun can be quite strong in summer, even though it's cloudy.
- There is only one café on the festival site. The food is very expensive.
- You will be walking long distances, so you need to carry as little as possible.

Interaction 4   page 34

d   Listen to your partner's problem and give advice. Then tell your partner about your problem. Listen to your partner's advice and accept or reject it. Use the Interaction language to help you.

Your problem: You are worried about a friend. He/She has started to meet lots of new friends online through a social network site. He/She spends hours chatting to them and now wants to travel to meet them. You don't think it's safe.

Interaction 5 page 44

c Work with a partner. Discuss what different things make a school better. You can use the ideas in the box but add some of your own ideas.

> a theatre   a laptop for every student   a music studio   good science labs
> a café with relaxing music   a swimming pool

d Now work in your group of four. Decide on the two most important things to include in a new school. Interrupt the other people in the group if necessary. Use the Interaction language to help you.

Interaction 6 page 52

c You are going to take part in three debates. Before you start, write down some ideas to support your opinions. During the debates use the Interaction language to help you agree and disagree.

1 Reality TV is great television. You disagree. Your partner agrees.
2 Being famous is wonderful. You agree. Your partner disagrees.
3 Hard work is more important than natural talent. You disagree. Your partner agrees.

d Have a discussion about the topics with your real opinions.

Interaction 7 page 62

c Laura, a girl in your class, hasn't come to school for the last three days. Your partner is going to guess what happened. Tell him/her if his/her ideas might be right. Use the Interaction language to help you.

<u>You know that:</u>

Laura never makes excuses to miss tests.

She likes most school subjects and being with her friends at school.

She was going to go skateboarding four days ago.

She often goes to stay with her grandparents, who live a long way from the school.

She usually keeps in touch by phone and email, but she hasn't contacted you.

Her sister had flu last week.

d There was a big party at the weekend, but the most popular boy in the class, Kevin, didn't go. Your partner is a friend of Kevin's and he/she will help you guess what might have happened to him. Use the Interaction language to help you.

Interaction 8 page 70

c Listen to your partner's explanations of how to use two gadgets. Ask for more information if you don't understand the explanations. Use the Interaction language to help you.

d Now look at the descriptions of the gadgets below and think about how they might work. Then explain to your partner how to use the gadgets and answer any questions he/she has. Use the Interaction language to help you.

- A gadget to help you find shops in your local area.
- A gadget to help you find your mobile phone.

Interaction 9 page 80

c Look at the information and act out the conversations with your partner. Use the Interaction language to help you.

Conversation 1: You have bought some new clothes (you decide what). You love them and show your friend. Ask your friend if he/she likes your new clothes. You start the conversation.

Conversation 2: Your friend has bought you a present. You hate it, but you don't want to hurt his/her feelings so you tell some white lies to be tactful. Your partner starts the conversation.

Interaction 10 page 88

c You are going to an Arts Festival together next weekend. You need to check some details. Use the Interaction language to help you.

Student B

	Saturday	Sunday
Morning	**What?** .... **Where?** The Orange Store **Cost?**	**What?** Manga exhibition with animated film clips **Where?** The Fitz Museum **Cost?** ....
Afternoon	**What?** Comedy (play) about university students **Where?** .... **Cost?** £7	**What?** .... **Where?** Odeon Cinema **Cost?** Free
Evening	**What?** .... **Where?** Sports Stadium **Cost?**	**What?** Party with writers and musicians **Where?** .... **Cost?** ....

Interaction 11 page 98

c Look at the information and act out the conversations with your partner. Use the Interaction language to help you.

Conversation 1: Your teacher gave you permission to borrow the class video camera to record something for a project. You took it home but it got broken (you decide how it happened). Your teacher wants to talk to you. Apologise and explain what happened. You start the conversation.

Conversation 2: You are a teacher. One of your students didn't come to your class yesterday and missed an important exam. Talk to the student and find out why he/she didn't come to your class. Decide on what should happen. Your partner starts the conversation.

Interaction 12 page 106

c Look at the information and act out the conversations with your partner. Try to find solutions to the problems. Use the Interaction language to help you.

Conversation 1: You are working on a school project together. Your partner had all the information saved on a laptop and it has just broken. The whole project is lost! You are angry and think it's your partner's fault as she/he should have made a back-up copy.

Conversation 2: You are preparing an outdoor party to celebrate the end of the school year. The party is in three days' time. The weather forecast predicts rain and storms. You don't believe in weather forecasts! You want to go ahead with the party as planned.

Speaking activities

Unit 1, page 8

Student B
Complete the questions with the correct form of the phrasal verbs and expressions. Then ask and answer the questions.

get   get into   get on with   get text messages   get through

1 How often do you .... ?
2 What did you .... for your last birthday?
3 Who don't you .... in your family?
4 What do you do to help you .... difficult exams?
5 Would you like to .... university? Why? / Why not?

Unit 7, page 59: Student A

Pictures A and C:
A This is a picture of a man called Chito playing with Pocho, a giant crocodile. They became friends 20 years ago in Costa Rica when Chito found Pocho close to death and looked after him for six months. Now they both perform for tourists.
C This is a close-up photo of a dragonhead eumegalodon, a type of cricket. Biochemist and photographer Igor Siwanowicz spent years photographing amazing images of insects in his home studio in Munich, Germany.

Unit 9, page 77

Picture A is real. Some cats (and some people) really do have different-coloured eyes.

Picture B is real. It was taken on a beach. The man is standing further away than the woman, which makes him look much smaller.

Picture C is a real watermelon. Watermelons are sometimes grown in boxes to make them square, so that they are easier to store and pack.

Picture D is also real. The woman is bending forwards, looking in her bag, and the angle the photo was taken from makes it impossible to see any of her head.

Unit 5, page 41

a **Student B**
Read the instructions and write words or numbers in the shapes.

1 In the triangle write the name of the most interesting teacher you have.
2 In the square write the subjects you have got high marks in so far this term.
3 In the circle write your favourite school day of the week.
4 In the rectangle write the number of minutes you spend doing your homework in the evening.
5 In the oval write the subject you like the least.

b Look at your partner's shapes and guess what the words or numbers mean. Ask follow-up questions if possible.

B: ⋯⟩ *7. Is that the number of lessons you have in one day?*
A: *No, it isn't. Try again.*

Unit 7, page 59: Student B

Pictures B and D:
B There are many different ways of 'sawing someone in half'. These include using two different people, boxes with secret sections inside, mirrors and false legs and feet.
D This is a zorse or zebrula. Its parents were a zebra and a horse. The zorse is more like a horse than a zebra in shape, but it has striped legs and it often has stripes on its body and neck.

Wordlist

(adj) = adjective   (adv) = adverb   (adv ph) = adverbial phrase
(n) = noun   (npl) = plural noun   (v) = verb   (pp) = past participle

Unit 1

Fitness
active (adj) /ˈæktɪv/
energetic (adj) /ˌenəˈdʒetɪk/
fit (adj) /fɪt/
flexible (adj) /ˈfleksɪbl/
stretch (v) /stretʃ/
train (v) /treɪn/
warm up (v) /ˌwɔːm ˈʌp/
work out (v) /ˌwɜːk ˈaʊt/

Phrasal verbs and expressions with *get*
get into (v) /ˌget ˈɪntə/
get on with someone (v) /ˌget ˈɒn wɪð ˌsʌmwʌn/
get on with something (v) /ˌget ˈɒn wɪð ˌsʌmθɪŋ/
get out of (v) /ˌget ˈaʊt əv/
get something across (v) /ˌget ˌsʌmθɪŋ əˈkrɒs/
get through (v) /ˌget ˈθruː/

Unit 2

Electrical items
dishwasher (n) /ˈdɪʃˌwɒʃə/
electric razor (n) /ɪˌlektrɪk ˈreɪzə/
food processor (n) /ˈfuːd ˌprəʊsesə/
freezer (n) /ˈfriːzə/
hairdryer (n) /ˈheəˌdraɪər/
microwave (n) /ˈmaɪkrəweɪv/
toaster (n) /ˈtəʊstə/
tumble dryer (n) /ˈtʌmbl ˌdraɪə/
vacuum cleaner (n) /ˈvækjuːm ˌkliːnə/
washing machine (n) /ˈwɒʃɪŋ məʃiːn/

Prefixes
overpriced (adj) /ˌəʊvəˈpraɪst/
oversleep (v) /ˌəʊvəˈsliːp/
overweight (adj) /ˌəʊvəˈweɪt/
precooked (adj) /ˌpriːˈkʊkt/
preheat (v) /ˌpriːˈhiːt/
pre-paid (adj) /ˌpriːˈpeɪd/
recharge (v) /ˌriːˈtʃɑːdʒ/
retake (v) /ˌriːˈteɪk/
reuse (v) /ˌriːˈjuːz/
supermarket (n) /ˈsuːpəˌmɑːkɪt/
supermodel (n) /ˈsuːpəˌmɒdl/
superpower (n) /ˈsuːpəˌpaʊə/

under-age (adj) /ˌʌndəˈreɪdʒ/
underground (n) /ˌʌndəˈgraʊnd/
underpaid (adj) /ˌʌndəˈpeɪd/

Unit 3

Natural disasters
avalanche (n) /ˈævəlɑːnʃ/
drought (n) /draʊt/
earthquake (n) /ˈɜːθkweɪk/
flood (n) /flʌd/
heat wave (n) /ˈhiːt weɪv/
hurricane (n) /ˈhʌrɪkən/
tsunami (n) /tsuːˈnɑːmi/
volcanic eruption (n) /vɒlˌkænɪk ɪˈrʌpʃn/

Outdoor clothes and equipment
anorak (n) /ˈænəræk/
fleece (n) /fliːs/
goggles (npl) /ˈgɒglz/
insect repellent (n) /ˈɪnsekt rɪˌpelənt/
rucksack (n) /ˈrʌksæk/
sleeping bag (n) /ˈsliːpɪŋ ˌbæg/
sun cream (n) /ˈsʌn ˌkriːm/
torch (n) /tɔːtʃ/
walking boots (npl) /ˈwɔːkɪŋ ˌbuːts/
wetsuit (n) /ˈwetsuːt/

Unit 4

Friends
be cross with someone (v) /bi ˈkrɒs wɪð ˌsʌmwʌn/
fall out with someone (v) /ˌfɔːl ˈaʊt wɪð ˌsʌmwʌn/
get on well with someone (v) /get ˈɒn ˈwel wɪð ˌsʌmwʌn/
have an argument with someone (v) /hæv ən ˈɑːgjʊmənt wɪð ˌsʌmwʌn/
keep in touch with someone (v) /ˌkiːp ɪn ˈtʌtʃ wɪð ˌsʌmwʌn/
let somebody down (v) /ˌlet sʌmbədi ˈdaʊn/
make up with someone (v) /ˌmeɪk ˈʌp wɪð ˌsʌmwʌn/
stick up for someone/something (v) /ˌstɪk ˈʌp fə ˌsʌmwʌn/ /ˌsʌmθɪŋ/

tell on someone (v) /ˈtel ɒn ˌsʌmwʌn/
chatty (adj) /ˈtʃæti/
cheeky (adj) /ˈtʃiːki/
fun (adj) /fʌn/
helpful (adj) /ˈhelpfəl/
laid-back (adj) /ˌleɪdˈbæk/
moody (adj) /ˈmuːdi/
outgoing (adj) /ˌaʊtˈgəʊɪŋ/
polite (adj) /pəˈlaɪt/
rude (adj) /ruːd/
sympathetic (adj) /ˌsɪmpəˈθetɪk/

Unit 5

School
be in detention (v) /bi ɪn dɪˈtenʃən/
cheat (v) /tʃiːt/
come top in (v) /kʌm ˈtɒp ˌɪn/
fail (v) /feɪl/
a high mark (n) /ə ˈhaɪ ˌmɑːk/
pass (v) /pɑːs/
retake (v) /ˌriːˈteɪk/
revise (v) /rɪˈvaɪz/
skive off (informal) (v) /ˌskaɪv ˈɒf/
term (n) /tɜːm/

Memory
forget (v) /fəˈget/
learn by heart (v) /ˌlɜːn baɪ ˈhɑːt/
memorise (v) /ˈmeməraɪz/
memory (n) /ˈmeməri/
mind (n) /maɪnd/
remind (v) /rɪˈmaɪnd/

Unit 6

Noun suffixes
appearance (n) /əˈpɪərəns/
artist (n) /ˈɑːtɪst/
creation (n) /kriˈeɪʃn/
creativity (n) /ˌkriːeɪˈtɪvɪti/
designer (n) /dɪˈzaɪnə/
entertainment (n) /entəˈteɪnmənt/
excitement (n) /ɪkˈsaɪtmənt/
exhibition (n) /ˌeksɪˈbɪʃən/
finalist (n) /ˈfaɪnəlɪst/
perfomance (n) /pəˈfɔːməns/
performer (n) /pəˈfɔːmə/
reality (n) /riˈælɪti/
selection (n) /sɪˈlekʃn/
singer (n) /ˈsɪŋə/
stylist (n) /ˈstaɪlɪst/

Entertainment collocations

art museum (n) /ˈɑːt mjuːˌziːəm/
fashion designer (n) /ˈfæʃn dɪˌzaɪnər/
media attention (n) /ˈmiːdiə əˌtenʃn/
natural talent (n) /ˌnætʃrl ˈtælənt/
prize money (n) /ˈpraɪz ˌmʌni/
reality TV (n) /riˈælɪti tiːˌviː/
sports star (n) /ˈspɔːts ˌstɑː/
studio audience (n) /ˌstjuːdiəʊ ˈɔːdiəns/
talent show (n) /ˈtælnt ˌʃəʊ/
world champion (n) /ˌwɜːld ˈtʃæmpiən/

Unit 7

Extreme adjectives

awful (adj) /ˈɔːfəl/
boiling (adj) /ˈbɔɪlɪŋ/
exhausted (adj) /ɪgˈzɔːstɪd/
freezing (adj) /ˈfriːzɪŋ/
huge (adj) /hjuːdʒ/
starving (adj) /ˈstɑːvɪŋ/
terrifying (adj) /ˈterəfaɪɪŋ/
tiny (adj) /ˈtaɪni/
unbelievable (adj) /ˌʌnbɪˈliːvəbl/

Phrasal verbs with go

go after (v) /gəʊ ˈɑːftə/
go away (v) /gəʊ əˈweɪ/
go back (v) /gəʊ ˈbæk/
go on (v) /gəʊ ˈɒn/
go out (v) /gəʊ ˈaʊt/
go over (v) /gəʊ ˈəʊvə/
go round (v) /gəʊ ˈraʊnd/
go through (v) /gəʊ ˈθruː/

Unit 8

Health problems

cold (n) /kəʊld/
cough (n) /kɒf/
dizzy (adj) /ˈdɪzi/
flu (n) /fluː/
headache (n) /ˈhedeɪk/
to hurt (v) /tə ˈhɜːt/
a pain in her chest (n) /ə ˈpeɪn ɪn hə ˌtʃest/
sick (adj) /sɪk/
sore throat (n) /ˈsɔː θrəʊt/
temperature (n) /ˈtemprətʃə/

Technology

cable (n) /ˈkeɪbl/
games console (n) /ˈgeɪmz ˌkɒnsəʊl/
GPS (global positioning system) (n) /ˌdʒiːpiːˈes/ /ˈgləʊbl pəˈzɪʃnɪŋ ˌsɪstəm/
memory card (n) /ˈmeməri kɑːd/

plug in (v) /ˌplʌg ˈɪn/
run out of battery (v) /rʌn ˌaʊt əv ˈbætri/
touch screen (n) /ˈtʌtʃ ˌskriːn/
voice-activated (adj) /ˈvɔɪsˌæktɪveɪtɪd/

Unit 9

Adjectives of opinion

amusing (adj) /əˈmjuːzɪŋ/
annoying (adj) /əˈnɔɪɪŋ/
confusing (adj) /kənˈfjuːzɪŋ/
depressing (adj) /dɪˈpresɪŋ/
fascinating (adj) /ˈfæsɪneɪtɪŋ/
gorgeous (adj) /ˈgɔːdʒəs/
hideous (adj) /ˈhɪdiəs/
impressive (adj) /ɪmˈpresɪv/
shocking (adj) /ˈʃɒkɪŋ/
upsetting (adj) /ʌpˈsetɪŋ/

Truth and lies

fake (adj) /feɪk/
fool somebody (v) /ˈfuːl sʌmbədi/
forge (v) /fɔːdʒ/
lies (npl) /laɪz/
the truth (n) /ðə ˈtruːθ/
trick (n) /trɪk/
truthful (adj) /ˈtruːθfl/
white lie (n) /ˌwaɪt ˈlaɪ/

Unit 10

Reading materials

autobiography (n) /ˌɔːtəbaɪˈɒgrəfi/
biography (n) /baɪˈɒgrəfi/
e-book (n) /ˈiːbʊk/
graphic novel (n) /ˌgræfɪk ˈnɒvl/
non-fiction (n) /nɒnˈfɪkʃən/
novel (n) /ˈnɒvl/
screenplay (n) /ˈskriːnpleɪ/
thriller (n) /ˈθrɪlə/

Adverbs and adverbial phrases

at first (adv) /ət ˈfɜːst/
at the beginning (adv ph) /ət ðə bɪˈgɪnɪŋ/
in the end (adv ph) /ɪn ðə ˈend/
luckily (adv) /ˈlʌkəli/
meanwhile (adv) /ˈmiːnwaɪl/
one night (adv ph) /wʌn ˈnaɪt/
soon afterwards (adv) /ˌsuːn ˈɑːftəwədz/
suddenly (adv) /ˈsʌdənli/
surprisingly (adv) /səˈpraɪzɪŋli/
unfortunately (adv) /ʌnˈfɔːtʃənətli/
while (adv) /waɪl/

Unit 11

Crime

bank robbery (n) /ˈbæŋk ˌrɒbəri/
burglary (n) /ˈbɜːgləri/
hacking (n) /ˈhækɪŋ/
identity theft (n) /aɪˈdentɪti ˌθeft/
piracy (n) /ˈpaɪrəsi/
plagiarism (n) /ˈpleɪdʒərɪzm/
shoplifting (n) /ˈʃɒpˌlɪftɪŋ/
theft (n) /θeft/
vandalism (n) /ˈvændəlɪzm/

Crime collocations

charge (v) /tʃɑːdʒ/
community service (n) /kəˌmjuːnəti ˈsɜːvɪs/
fine (n) /faɪn/
law (n) /lɔː/
prison (n) /ˈprɪzn/
record (n) /ˈrekɔːd/
sentence (n) /ˈsentəns/
suspect (n) /ˈsʌspekt/
youth (n) /juːθ/

Unit 12

Hopes and ambitions

achieve (v) /əˈtʃiːv/
aim (v) /eɪm/
ambition (n) /æmˈbɪʃn/
challenge (n) /ˈtʃælɪndʒ/
expect (v) /ɪkˈspekt/
goal (n) /gəʊl/
hope (v) /həʊp/

verbs with dependent prepositions

be good or bad at (v) /bi ˈgʊd ət/ /bi ˈbæd ət/
be interested in (v) /bi ˈɪntrəstɪd ɪn/
be keen on (v) /bi ˈkiːn ɒn/
concentrate on (v) /ˈkɒnsəntreɪt ɒn/
decide on (v) /dɪˈsaɪd ɒn/
depend on (v) /dɪˈpend ɒn/
listen to (v) /ˈlɪsən tu/
look forward to (v) /lʊk ˈfɔːwəd tə/
make progress in (v) /meɪk ˈprəʊgres ɪn/
succeed in (v) /səkˈsiːd ɪn/

Irregular verbs

Verb	Past simple	Past participle	Verb	Past simple	Past participle
be	was/were	been	lose	lost	lost
become	became	become	make	made	made
begin	began	begun	mean	meant	meant
blow	blew	blown	meet	met	met
break	broke	broken	pay	paid	paid
bring	brought	brought	put	put	put
build	built	built	read	read	read
burn	burned/burnt	burned/burnt	ride	rode	ridden
buy	bought	bought	ring	rang	rung
can	could	been able	run	ran	run
catch	caught	caught	say	said	said
choose	chose	chosen	see	saw	seen
come	came	come	sell	sold	sold
cost	cost	cost	send	sent	sent
cut	cut	cut	set	set	set
do	did	done	shake	shook	shaken
draw	drew	drawn	shoot	shot	shot
drink	drank	drunk	shut	shut	shut
drive	drove	driven	sing	sang	sung
eat	ate	eaten	sit	sat	sat
fall	fell	fallen	sleep	slept	slept
feel	felt	felt	speak	spoke	spoken
fight	fought	fought	spell	spelled/spelt	spelled/spelt
find	found	found	spend	spent	spent
fly	flew	flown	spin	span/spun	spun
forget	forgot	forgotten	stand	stood	stood
get	got	got	steal	stole	stolen
give	gave	given	strike	struck	struck
go	went	gone/been	swim	swam	swum
grow	grew	grown	swing	swung	swung
have	had	had	take	took	taken
hear	heard	heard	teach	taught	taught
hit	hit	hit	tell	told	told
hold	held	held	think	thought	thought
hurt	hurt	hurt	throw	threw	thrown
keep	kept	kept	understand	understood	understood
know	knew	known	wake	woke	woken
learn	learned/learnt	learned/learnt	wear	wore	worn
leave	left	left	win	won	won
lend	lent	lent	write	wrote	written
let	let	let			

Phonemic chart

Consonant sounds

 /b/ bird

 /tʃ/ cheese

 /d/ door

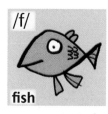 /f/ fish

 /g/ girl

 /h/ heart

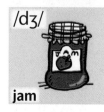 /dʒ/ jam

 /k/ key

 /l/ leaf

 /m/ monkey

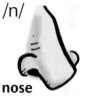 /n/ nose

 /ŋ/ ring

 /p/ pen

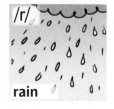 /r/ rain

 /s/ sofa

 /ʃ/ shoe

 /ʒ/ television

 /t/ table

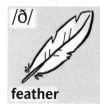 /ð/ feather

 /θ/ think

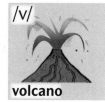 /v/ volcano

 /w/ window

 /j/ yoga

 /z/ zoo

Vowel sounds

 /æ/ apple

 /e/ head

 /ɪ/ insect

 /ɒ/ hot

 /ʌ/ umbrella

 /ʊ/ book

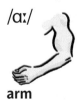 /ɑː/ arm

 /ɜː/ earth

 /iː/ sheep

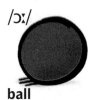 /ɔː/ ball

 /uː/ moon

 /eə/ chair

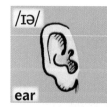 /ɪə/ ear

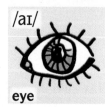 /aɪ/ eye

 /eɪ/ paper

 /ɔɪ/ boy

 /əʊ/ phone

 /aʊ/ owl

 /ə/ computer

Go to the Interactive website for more pronunciation practice!

http://interactive.cambridge.org